Machine Learning-Based Prediction and Analysis of Student Examination Performance

Author:
Bhor

Chapter 1

Introduction

Student performance analysis in examinations using machine learning is a growing area of interest within the educational sector. This approach leverages advanced algorithms and data analysis techniques to predict, evaluate, and improve student outcomes based on various factors. Analysing student performance is crucial for a variety of stakeholders in the educational ecosystem, including educators, administrators, students, and policymakers. By understanding individual strengths and weaknesses, educators can customize learning experiences to meet the needs of each student.

With the advent of data-driven technologies, machine learning (ML) has emerged as a powerful tool for analysing and predicting student performance based on various influencing parameters. This personalized approach can enhance student engagement and improve learning outcomes. Analysis helps in developing adaptive learning technologies that adjust content delivery based on student performance, ensuring that each student is challenged appropriately. Performance data can help identify students who are at risk of failing or dropping out. Early detection allows for timely interventions such as tutoring, counselling, or additional resources. Educational institutions can implement support systems for students facing academic, social, or emotional challenges, ensuring that no student falls through the cracks [1][2]. Institution can allocate resources more effectively by identifying areas where they are most needed. For example, additional support can be directed towards subjects or student groups that are struggling.

Data-driven insights can inform budget planning and ensure that funds are used in ways that have the greatest impact on student achievement. Analysing performance data helps in assessing the effectiveness of the current curriculum. It can highlight areas where the curriculum is strong and areas that need improvement. Educators can make informed decisions about curriculum changes, ensuring that it remains relevant and meets the evolving needs of students. Performance data can provide insights into teaching effectiveness. Identifying best practices and areas for improvement can inform professional development programs. Professional development can be tailored based on the analysis, focusing on areas where teachers need the most support. Regular performance analysis provides students with feedback on their progress. Constructive feedback can motivate students to improve and take ownership of their learning. Clear data on performance helps students set realistic and achievable goals, fostering a growth mind set. Policymakers can use performance data to develop and implement educational policies that address the specific needs of schools and students. Performance analysis ensures accountability at all levels of the education system. Institutions and educators can be held accountable for student outcomes, promoting a culture of continuous improvement.

Analysing performance data helps in identifying achievement gaps between different student groups. Understanding these disparities is the first step in addressing them. Institutions can implement strategies to ensure that all students, regardless of their background, have equal opportunities to succeed. Performance analysis provides parents with detailed information about their child's progress, enabling them to be more involved in their education. Educational institutions can work with parents to develop strategies that support student learning at home, creating a more holistic approach to education. Performance data can guide students in making informed decisions about their future education and career paths. It helps in identifying areas of interest and

potential career opportunities. Analysis helps in identifying the skills that students need to develop to be successful in the future, ensuring that they are prepared for the demands of the workforce. Analysing student performance is a multifaceted process that benefits all stakeholders in the educational system. It drives personalized learning, supports early interventions, optimizes resource allocation, informs curriculum development, enhances teacher training, boosts student motivation, shapes policy making, promotes equity, engages parents, and prepares students for future success.

Machine learning (ML) refers to a set of techniques that allow computers to learn from data and make predictions or decisions [3][4]. In my thesis to analyse student performance in examination machine learning can be used to predict student grades based on historical data. Identify factors influencing student performance. Classify students into different performance categories. Recommend personalized study plans and interventions. The machine learning techniques used is linear regression which is the type of supervised learning [5]. Linear regression is used for predicting continuous outcomes like exam scores. After this comes the training part which involves the process of feeding the model with training data and adjusting its parameters to minimize the difference between the predicted outputs and the actual labels. The last steps is the testing and validation which evaluate the model's performance on a separate dataset. Effective ML models rely on high-quality data. Relevant data for student performance analysis include demographic Information like gender, socioeconomic status. Academic records like grades, test preparation coursework. The application of machine learning in analysing student performance in examinations offers significant potential for enhancing educational outcomes. By leveraging advanced data analysis techniques, educators can gain deeper insights into student learning processes, leading to more informed decision-making and better support for students. As the field continues to evolve, addressing the associated challenges will be key to realizing the full benefits of this technology in education.

The primary goal of this thesis is to explore the application of machine learning techniques in predicting student performance in examinations. The study aims to identify key factors affecting student performance, compare various ML algorithms, and evaluate their predictive accuracy. Additionally, the research will focus on developing a predictive model that can assist educators in early intervention strategies.

This thesis is structured as follows:

Chapter 1 provides an overview of the research background, problem statement, objectives, and significance of the study.

Chapter 2 reviews the related literature on student performance prediction and the use of machine learning in education.

Chapter 3 gives the idea about the conceptual frameworkwhich is the outlines of the research methodology, including data collection, pre-processing, and selection of machine learning models.

Chapter 4describe the plan and procedure of the study that presents the experimental results, model evaluation, and comparison of different algorithms.

Chapter 5is the analysis of data

Chapter 6 discusses about the findings and interpretation of data

Chapter 7 discusses about the industrial and potential applications of the study.

Chapter 8 concludes the thesis with key takeaways, limitations, and suggestions for future research.

This study aims to contribute to the field of educational data mining and provide actionable insights for improving student performance in examinations.

Chapter 2

Literature Review

The significance of analysing student performance in exams for educational institutions and policy makers. The emergence of machine learning as a valuable tool for analysing large volumes of exam data. Statement of the research objectives and scope of the literature review. Overview of commonly used machine learning algorithms for student performance analysis, including decision trees, logistic regression, random forests, and neural networks. Explanation of how each algorithm is applied to predict student outcomes, identify patterns, and extract insights from exam data. Performance Metrics in Student Performance Analysis. Description of performance metrics such as accuracy, precision, recall, F1-score, and area under the ROC curve. Illustrative examples of how these metrics are used to evaluate the performance of machine learning models in predicting student performance in exams.

Factors Affecting Student Performance by examining of factors influencing student performance, including demographic variables (e.g., age, gender, ethnicity), academic background (e.g., GPA, prior coursework), and socio-economic status. Discussion of how machine learning models incorporate these factors to make predictions about student outcomes. Applications and Case Studies to review of real-world applications and case studies where machine learning techniques have been applied to analyse student performance in exams. Comparative analysis of different machine learning approaches used for student performance analysis. Identification of challenges in student performance analysis using machine learning techniques, such as data quality issues, model interpretability, and scalability. Discussion of future research directions, including the integration of additional data sources (e.g., student behavior data), development of personalized learning interventions, and exploration of ethical considerations. Summary of key findings from the literature review. Emphasis on the potential of machine learning techniques to enhance our understanding of student performance in exams and inform educational practices.

Several studies have been conducted to investigate the factors affecting student's performance using learning analytics and machine learning techniques. Academic determinants such as student qualification, parental education, their nourishment and their IQ level analysis by reading, writing and learning scores have affected student performance.

This review is used to analyse student's performance in exam using machine learning based on past research in this field. It also identifies strengths in the existing literature and highlights the unique contribution that the study makes to learning analytics.

In one of the research stated by Kasi et. al. (2020) concluded that it is important to examine the factors that impact students' academic performance as it can improve teaching and learning processes [6]. Numerous academic and non-academic facets affect student performance, such as study time, frequency of absences, recreational activities, and interpersonal relationships. Educational data mining (EDM) and learning analytics (LA) are two closely related fields that reveal useful information from educational databases to generate actionable insights.

The research and finding done by Durga et. al. (2020) stated that student's scores across few important measures that tries to determine their academic excellence such as subjects conceptual knowledge based on marks scored in that exam, time management skills based on number of questions attempted is obtained priory, have been used to create homogeneous groups of students who opted for same subjects and share perceptions of their non-cognitive abilities [7]. Result of statistical graphical data helps students and teachers to track the performance and direction in which the students perception and knowledge regarding the subject is inculcated. The results indicate the degree to which specific profiles predict outcome of the conceptually relevant data and widen the scope of their information to discover knowledge from data. Also it facilitates smooth and efficient handling of data that includes storage and modification of data in files which can be easily converted to other formats as desired by the user.

The study found out by Reddy et. al. (2021) that automation to do mundane tasks and the expectations for students already equipped with good programming skills is on the rise [8]. In parallel, there have been a rising number of students who find it difficult to attain the skills necessary in order to get the dream IT job they desire. So they did the work to bridge the gap between the employer and the future employee of the company by the use of Student Performance Analysis System (SPAS) at college level. SPAS is an online web application system which enables students to know prior hand if their level of skills for the placement is enough to get placed or not, given the necessary inputs. SPAS have an intelligent learning algorithm which utilizes a rich database, analyses the records of previous student's traits and develops a model for further prediction. The performance evaluation of students by SPAS is by the cumulative predictor algorithm involving generation of several random forest trees on the available data. SPAS learn and create its model reaching higher accuracy with increasing data availability.

In one of the study Karthikeyan et. al.(2021) states that academic output of the student is normally stored in various formats in the student administration system (files, documents, records, photographs and other formats) [9]. These data can be collected for valuable knowledge from the students. However, it is difficult to analyse the increasing amount of data of students through conventional statistical techniques and database management tools. For universities to gather valuable information, a tool is therefore required. This helpful knowledge can be used to predict the success of students. The analysis learning results is a framework that aims for success in the areas of student interest at various levels and dimensions. Their work proposes a complete structure as a rule-based recommendation method not only for analysing and forecasting the success of students but also for presenting their reasons. Their system analyses demographic details for pupils, studies and psychological features so that students, teachers and parents can collect all possible knowledge. To seek maximum accuracy in academic predictions across a range of powerful techniques of data mining the system successfully recognizes the limitations of the student and makes adequate recommendations.

The data clustering technique named k-means clustering which is applied to analyse student's learning behaviour which have been stated byJirage et. al. (2015). The student's evaluation factor like class quizzes, mid and final exam assignment are studied. It is recommended that all these correlated information should be conveyed to the class adviser before the conduction of final examination [10]. That study will help the teachers to reduce the drop out ratio to a significant level and improve the performance of student.

In one of the study Prajapati et. al (2017)did the survey of existing tools and techniques that have been designed [11]. Their work concluded that the main concern of the teachers regarding the performance issue of the students is covered by introducing the analysis tool R. This analysis tool R uses machine learning approaches like Naive Bayes, K-Nearest Neighbors (KNN) first for building a model. Their work suggests that one should use the cognitive modelling for designing the knowledge-based so that they can produce better results.

The study and research of Anusha et. al. (2019) mainly focused in their work on quality and value of the student's advancement in his profession as a challenge or an inquiry. These organizations centre on quality in training consistently countless alumni from schools and colleges, as for the information gathered from the criticism of students, order an information mining strategy is connected to it [12]. It is a stage to examine the elements influencing the performance of students so as to assess the present understudy execution and make proficient strides in the expectation of the no doubt happening connections between the different parts of learning and to upgrade the nature of instruction in future and help the educational organizers to design in like manner.

In one of the studies Kumar et. al.(2019) have used the combination of K-Means clustering algorithm with Artificial Neural Network(ANN) and Support Vector Machine(SVM) classification algorithm to evaluate the student performance in order to reduce the human effort [13]. The evaluation is done on the basis of Mean Square Error and Effort Estimation. The results of their implementation shows that the performance of Artificial Neural Network in comparison to Support Vector Machine is better. The Mean Square Error is 5-20% better whereas the Effort Estimation is around

15-27% better. The future possibilities include changing the total number of neurons or varying the satisfying parameters.

In one of the study Naveen et. al.(2022) have explored the machine learning algorithm on e-learning data has been proposed as a useful method to compare student's performance as well as supporting certain prediction [14]. The performance evaluation of machine learning algorithm is also compared to determine the effectiveness for the task. This prediction can benefit teacher and course planner learns how to increase student's results in the university exam. They have used cycle test mark, model mark as data sets. While for prediction techniques, the classification method is frequently used in educational data mining area. Under the classification techniques, Neural Network and Decision Tree are the two methods used for predicting student's performance. Their future scope is that the system can be implemented as a web based application and android application so that the many of the institution may get benefits by using this system and many more features can be added which are related to school.

In one of the findings Pallathadka et. al. (2021) anticipated that student's talents and interests might be linked to their performance. A teacher's success is frequently measured by the performance of his students. Their work deal with data analysis from students and teachers [15]. The analysis might be used to categorize or forecast machine learning algorithms such as Nave Bayes, ID3, C4.5, and Support Vector Machines (SVMs) which are a popular supervised learning algorithm used for classification and regression tasks. These algorithms are being researched in the experimental investigation. A data set of UCI machinery student performance is employed. Algorithms are evaluated based on characteristics such as accuracy and error rate. SVM is the most accurate technique for classifying a data set and analysing student's performance.

In one of the study Acharya et. al. (2017) analysed the performance of the students and their attributes. The data set are derived by surveying a group of students of colleges it is to be noted that the developed research methodology is general in nature [16]. It could be applied to full time as well as distance education courses including the courses where web based learning is done. The training set contains 309 instances whereas the testing set contains 104 instances. After detailed analysis it was found that the most convenient algorithm to generate the set of production rules C4.5 was used to generate the decision tree. F-Measure and Kappa Statistic were used to determine the efficiency of the prediction algorithm. Average F-Measure value for the training dataset was found to be 0.79 whereas for the testing dataset was found to be 0.66. The later value seems to be slightly low perhaps due to the fact that the number of testing instances is only 104. Similar results are shown by Kappa Statistic also. Priya et. al. (2021) concluded that use of machine learning methods in conjunction with supervised learning algorithms better understand the efficiency of the algorithm with respect to student records, where they analyse student performance and classified it into three categories: high, medium, and poor, with a 79% precision [17]. They had some technological solutions in the future to increase the quality of student success. The user interface model was planned developed to automatically include student records and to send staff warning messages about students who are doing poorly. They used a neural network to construct the prediction and anticipate improved performance. Non-academic qualities should be combined with academic attributes.

In one study Dhilipan et. al. (2020) focuses on the student academic growth analysis using machine learning techniques. For analysis Binomial logical regression, Decision tree, Entropy and KNN classifier were used. That process can help the instructor to decide easily about performance of the students and schedule better method for improving their academics[19]. In future additional features were added to their dataset to acquire better accuracy.

Alshabandar et. al.(2020) depicts that two sets of exterminates have been carried out in their study using regression and classification analysis. The results of predicting student's assessments grades model shows that the student's performance in a particular assignment relies on student's mark in the previous assignment within single courses. The researchers conclude that student's prior grade point average (GPA) with a low mark is considered as a significant factor of withdrawal from the next course in the traditional classroom setting, The date of student deregistration from the course is a valuable predictor that is significantly correlated with student performance[20]. With the regression analysis, the data does not provide the last date of student's activity prior to undertaken assessments. The finding results have been recommended to take into account the temporal features on predicting of subsequent assessments grades. Future research direction involves the use of temporal features for predicting student's assessments grades model. With temporal feature time series analysis will be untaken might be more advanced machine learning will be utilized.

In the study of Kotaiah et. al.(2019) states that feature engineering, the method of transforming dataset for machine learning, is including an essential factor in propagating reliable prediction outcomes. Two diverse datasets were examined with three various machine learning techniques, and their outcomes were analysed applying for evaluation criteria. Techniques applied were Naïve Bayes classification, decision trees, and linear regression. For the computation of machine learning techniques, feature engineering was employed to the modified and raw version of the dataset individually. The central process of feature selection was feature engineering. In the state of regression and classification trees, supplementary feature engineering was prepared in the manner of custom feature production. Feature engineering was performed both with automatic interpretation and manual functionality of the dataset. In summation, features tuning was made with an error and trial strategy [21]. The outcome of both datasets shows differences and relationships with their employment in fundamental education. In the first dataset, the relationship is that recall value was frequently greater than the precision value. The variation was in the efficiency value. This can be connected to the various individualistic attributes. In the original analysis, the dependent attribute was not changed into binary valued attributes. Concluding the dependent attribute might have addressed the predictions carefully in the research. The second dataset, the primary analysis adopted an additional attribute that symbolizes the prior exam ranks and delivered better performance than from their studies. Though, once those attributes are neglected, accuracy rates were comparable to that paper.

In one of the study Kotaiah et. al.(2017) depicted that for predicting student's performance meta-analysis on predicting student's performance has motivated them to carry out further research to be applied in the proper environment [22]. It will help the educational system to monitor the students' performance in a systematic way.

The research examinedby Memon et. al.(2020) that a massive VLE(Virtual Learning Environment) based student behavioural dataset in terms of magnitude [23].Through literary studies of student behavioural studies, a master feature vector is created possessing influential properties controlling the student's behaviour. Two different analysis procedures further examine the feature vector, i.e., expert opinion is obtained for identifying procrastination tendencies. In parallel a similar feature vector was analysed for automatic pattern generation using K-means clustering. For an optimal number of cluster identification, the elbow method issued. A student behavioural dataset focusing on procrastination behaviour is proposed to represent enough of the problem domain in terms of the dataset size. The existing VLE dataset is enhanced by an additional label to each record that identifies procrastination in students interacting with VLEs. The procrastination dataset is further fed to the classifier following a detailed analysis protocol based on two algorithms. These classifiers are fine-tuned to get optimal performance accuracy. The best performer classifier hits the accuracy of 83.3%. In conclusion, the study was completed in the following aspects: 1) The proposal of procrastination related student behavioural dataset in terms of considerable size.2) Detailed steps in the form of algorithms for data formation and classification. 3) Detailed visualizations of clustering and classification to identify procrastination tendencies.

In one of the study by Gupta et. al.(2019) created an evaluation model was implemented using various machine learning techniques. A student dataset of 500 records is taken for training and testing of KNN, SVM, decision trees, Naïve Bayes and KNN supervised learning methods [24]. The work mainly focused on four primarily important features such as attendance, quiz, assignment and terms marks for evaluation of student's performance. These machine learning techniques classified the result data into three classes, namely excellent, good and improve. They also have compared these supervised learning techniques in terms of its accuracy rate and found SVM and KNN better as compared to others. As a further progress, two different directions were adopted. First, a larger dataset were considered for experiments and second, other machine learning techniques may be used for analysis.

In the study Mittal et. al. (2019) compared the outcomes of six different classifiers to identify those students who have high probability to have reappeared in some of the courses, by doing predictive analysis. The investigation in this paper differs from previous related works in respect that the authors compared the accuracy of six EDM(Educational Data Mining) techniques to identify those students, who are likely to have reappear in course at an early stage, so that action can be taken to minimize the rate of failure at the end of course[25]. Specifically, the six EDM techniques ("Naïve Bayes", "Logistic Regression", "Multilayer Perception", "Support Vector Machine", "J48 decision tree" and "Random Forest") were compared to conduct the study. The research results allows to conclude that the analysed classification algorithms are quite effective for early identification of those students who can have reappear in course, which can then be useful for parents or teachers to take a corrective action at an early stage. The prediction of student's performance can be done to a good extent by using the six features gender, caste, percentage, family income, mother's occupation and number of friends. The two classifiers, multi-layer perception and Random Forest prove to be the most appropriate classifiers for predicting student's performance. For future work, this analysis can be further taken forward by using data sets from different universities and also applying other data pre-processing techniques.

In one of the study Ravindra (2020) concluded that in the future AI will enable new capabilities to address library user's information needs. Libraries can use AI tools to provide not just information but deep intelligence offering Insight as a Service (IAAS). It is necessary to understand the advantages and disadvantages of artificial intelligence and machine learning for better use and its application in libraries and information centres. AI is impacting the way information is processed and searched for and information professionals will be able to use these exciting new technologies to enhance their services and help users find and access specific information more easily and quickly [26]. Library and information centres will get benefits by the development of the efficient expert system for technical services as well as for information processing and management.

The research aim of Lubna Mahmoud (2019) was to predict students' performance to improve its reputation and ranking by selecting high performing students to engage them in solving real world issues. The support vector machine classifier with radial kernel was the one which proved its efficiency (among the rest of classifiers) in predicting students' performance in all courses' grades, including their dissertation projects' grade. Moreover, another performance measure was used and it's called balanced accuracy. Balanced accuracy is an evaluation metric that takes the average of sensitivity (or recall) and specificity to calculate the accuracy rate of a certain attribute's class [27]. So, the balanced accuracy rate was extracted from the confusion matrix of the classification results of all tested classifiers. Then they were compared with the calculated accuracy baseline and the result has recorded the highest accuracy rates with values 79% and 77% for the classification of class A for, in respectively. Noting that, although SVM produced acceptable accuracy results, it is still susceptible more than LDA to be biased with imbalanced dataset observations while training the model. Kappa and balanced accuracy considered reliable metrics, but examining the efficiency of LDA and SVM Radial models with more evaluation and diagnostic metrics, like ROC Curve or F-Scores, will be an interesting topic for further investigation in the future. Overall, students' grades in most courses were correlated with students' grade is dissertation course (i.e. grade attribute in), however, students grade in course 1 and course 2 (i.e. grade1 and grade 2 attributes) were considered the highest key indicators for predicting students' performance in dissertation project (i.e. in predicting grade attribute). Moreover, the classification accuracy rates of LDA and SVM algorithms were the highest, and considered highly significant in comparison with the stated baseline .Another key findings, and unlike predicting grades in, the indication of the key attributes in classifying students grade in dissertation project (i.e. grade attribute) using visualization and clustering techniques were found much easier. Besides, LDA and SVM algorithms proved the importance of students' pre-admission records (like: student age) in predicting their performance in all their courses' grades (attribute grads in). That outcome was identified by evaluating the calculated accuracy rate of LDA and SVM classification algorithms that were significant and exceeded the calculated baseline. Despite that extracting the best indicators for predicting grades attribute in was difficult using the heat map (since the number of the attributes were very few in comparison to the number of instances), the indicators were easily identified using the dendrogram. Their research studied only students' administration records to form the classification models, ignoring by that other variables that could affect students' learning outcomes, like: attendance, instructor course delivery, and many others. That was because the main focus in this project was to explore the feasibility of utilizing from small dataset size in predicting student performance and to shed the light on the importance of visualization and dendrogram in identifying valuable predictors.

Kotsiantis, Pierrakeas, and Pintelas (2004) explored the potential of machine learning techniques in predicting student performance in university-level distance learning. The researchers highlighted the importance of such predictive models in identifying at-risk students, enabling timely intervention, and improving overall educational outcomes. They utilized key demographic characteristics and students' performance in written assignments as inputs for supervised machine learning algorithms [29].The study compared six state-of-the-art algorithms through two experiments using datasets provided by the Hellenic Open University. Among the algorithms evaluated, the Naïve Bayes algorithm emerged as the most suitable for developing a predictive support tool. It demonstrated high accuracy, exceptional sensitivity, and ease of implementation. These findings underline the value of integrating machine learning into educational settings, particularly in enhancing student support and performance monitoring systems.

The ultimate goal of any educational institution is offering the best educational experience and knowledge to the students. Identifying the students who need extra support and taking the appropriate actions to enhance their performance plays an important role in achieving that goal.

In the research done by Hussein Altabrawee et al(2019), four machine learning techniques have been used to build a classifier that can predict the performance of the students in a computer science subject that is offered by Al-Muthanna University (MU), College Of Humanities. The machine learning techniques include Artificial Neural Network, Naïve Bayes, Decision Tree, and Logistic Regression [30]. This research pays extra attention to the effect of using the internet as a learning resource and the effect of the time spent by students on social networks on the students' performance. These effects introduced by using features that measure whether the student uses the internet for learning and the time spent on the social networks by the students. The models have been compared using the ROC index performance measure and the classification accuracy. In addition, different measures have been computed such as the classification error, precision, recall, and the F measure. The dataset used to build the models is collected based on a survey given to the students and the students' grade book. The ANN (fully connected feed forward multilayer ANN) model achieved the best performance that is equal to 0.807 and achieved the best classification accuracy that is equal to 77.04%. In addition, the decision tree model identified five factors as important factors which influence the performance of the students.

Researchers from the Department of Computer Engineering, CEME, NUST, including Masood, Khan, Hussain, and Shaukat (2019), explored the predictive capabilities of machine learning models in the educational domain. They stated that Educational Data Mining (EDM) has emerged as a pivotal field in contemporary education research due to the increasing complexity of student challenges in the modern technological era. EDM aims to address these challenges by leveraging data-driven methodologies to support students effectively [31]. This review examines systematic approaches and advancements in EDM, focusing on studies conducted between 2012 and 2019.A systematic literature review (SLR) was performed to identify and analyse 20 significant studies within the domain of EDM. These studies highlight the application of 11 advanced machine learning models that have shown promise in addressing educational challenges. These models were applied to two publicly available student databases to predict future academic outcomes. To ensure effective predictions, feature extraction techniques were employed to pre-process the data. Subsequently, machine learning models were trained and evaluated on these databases. The performance of the models was compared using key metrics, including accuracy and F-measure, to identify the most effective model for predicting student outcomes. The results indicate that advanced machine learning techniques can play a crucial role in identifying at-risk students. By leveraging these predictive models, educators and institutions can implement timely interventions and targeted support to assist underperforming students. This review underscores the importance of EDM in modern education and highlights the potential of machine learning models to improve student success rates through data-driven insights.

Predicting students' academic performance has garnered significant attention in educational research due to its potential to facilitate timely pedagogical interventions and ensure satisfactory student outcomes. While existing literature extensively explores data-driven approaches for predicting performance in individual courses or problem-solving tasks, less focus has been given to predicting performance in completing degree programs[31]. Xu, Moon, and van der Schaar (2019) address this gap by developing a machine learning method tailored to tackle the unique challenges associated with degree completion prediction. These challenges include the diverse backgrounds and course selections of students, the varying in formativeness of courses for prediction, and the necessity of incorporating students' evolving academic progress. To overcome these obstacles, the proposed method introduces a bilayer predictive structure comprising multiple base predictors and a cascade of ensemble predictors. This structure enables dynamic tracking of students' evolving performance states. Additionally, a data-driven approach based on latent factor models and probabilistic matrix factorization is utilized to determine course relevance, thereby enhancing the accuracy of base predictors. The efficacy of this method was demonstrated through extensive simulations on a dataset of undergraduate students from UCLA, collected over three years. The results revealed that the proposed model outperformed benchmark approaches, establishing its potential for effective prediction of degree completion outcomes.This study underscores the importance of advanced machine learning techniques in addressing complex educational challenges and contributes to the growing body of research focused on improving academic success rates.

Aziz (2020) examined the application of machine learning and data mining techniques to predict student performance in educational settings. The study emphasized the critical role of predictive models in enhancing the success of educational processes. By leveraging data from school records, the research sought to uncover insights into student behaviour, the influence of key factors such as parental involvement, attendance, and age, and their impact on academic outcomes [32].The paper explored the use of machine learning algorithms, including Gradient Boosted Decision Trees (GBDT), Random Forest Decision Trees (RFDT), and deep learning methods, to analyse educational data. A comparative analysis of these algorithms provided insights into their effectiveness and the relative significance of various factors in predicting student performance. Aziz's findings underscore the potential of machine learning to optimize educational strategies and interventions by identifying key determinants of academic success.

Kim, Vizitei, and Ganapathi (Udacity, 2020) addressed the complex task of student performance prediction in the context of online education. They highlighted the importance of accurate early-stage predictions for enabling timely educational interventions, which can significantly improve learning outcomes. Despite the challenges of forecasting student performance, particularly during the initial stages of coursework, their study introduced a novel deep learning approach to this problem[33].The researchers reframed the prediction task as a sequential event prediction problem and proposed GritNet, a deep learning algorithm based on bidirectional long short-term memory (BLSTM). Using data from Udacity students, their results demonstrated that GritNet consistently outperformed traditional logistic regression methods. The algorithm was especially effective in making precise predictions within the first few weeks of a course, a critical period for intervention. This study underscores the potential of advanced deep learning techniques in improving the accuracy and timeliness of student performance predictions in online learning environments.

Orji and Vassileva(2020) investigated the critical role of student engagement in academic performance, particularly in technology-enhanced learning systems (TELS). Engagement, defined as the degree of passion, interest, and attention students exhibit in their learning environments, has traditionally been encouraged through teaching strategies such as active participation and focused attention [34]. However, with the increasing adoption of TELS in education, engagement strategies have evolved, prompting the need for research into effective methods of fostering engagement in online settings. This study explored student engagement by analysing activity logs from an undergraduate course in a TELS. These logs provided objective, unbiased data reflecting students' actual learning behaviours. The researchers employed supervised (Random Forest) and unsupervised (clustering) machine learning approaches to identify patterns in engagement and its relationship with academic performance, measured by final grade points. Their findings revealed that both engagement and assessment scores, derived from quizzes and assignments, are strong predictors of student academic performance. These insights emphasize the potential of data-driven interventions to enhance engagement and support student success in online learning environments.

Ghorbani and Ghousi (2020) explored the challenges of predicting student performance in educational settings, particularly focusing on the imbalanced nature of educational datasets. Predicting student performance has become an essential research area due to its potential to enhance educational outcomes. However, imbalanced datasets pose a significant challenge, as they often lead to biased predictive models [35].The study compared various resampling techniques, including Borderline SMOTE, Random Over Sampler, SMOTE, SMOTE-ENN, SVM-SMOTE, and SMOTE-Tomek, to address the issue of data imbalance. The researchers applied these methods to two distinct datasets and evaluated their performance using multiple machine learning classifiers, such as Random Forest, K-Nearest Neighbors, Artificial Neural Networks, XGBoost, Support Vector Machines, Decision Trees, Logistic Regression, and Naïve Bayes. Validation techniques like random hold-out and shuffle 5-fold cross-validation were employed to ensure robustness.Results showed that models perform better when datasets are balanced, and fewer classes with nominal features lead to improved predictive accuracy. Among the resampling techniques, SVM-SMOTE was identified as the most effective, while the Random Forest classifier delivered the best overall performance when combined with SVM-SMOTE. These findings underscore the importance of addressing data imbalance in educational data mining and highlight the effectiveness of advanced resampling techniques in improving the accuracy of predictive models.

Mehdi, et.al (2020) developed a performance analysis system focused on outcome-based learning. This system aims to excel across diverse dimensions by predicting and analysing students' academic performance. The framework leverages students' demographic, academic, and psychological data to extract valuable insights from various stakeholders, including students, teachers, and parents. The study employed advanced data mining techniques to achieve high accuracy in academic performance predictions [36]. By identifying students' weak points, the framework enables targeted interventions to support academic improvement. A case study conducted on 200 students demonstrated the proposed framework's superior performance compared to existing systems. These findings highlight the potential of integrating data-driven methods to optimize outcome-based learning and enhance student success.

Kabra and Bichkar conducted a study focusing on the performance prediction of engineering students using decision tree algorithms (2011). They analysed data to identify patterns influencing academic outcomes. Their research provides valuable insights into the application of machine learning techniques in educational contexts, emphasizing the effectiveness of decision trees for predictive modelling [37].Data mining has emerged as a valuable tool for decision-making in educational systems, offering insights that can inform and enhance learning strategies. Among the various methods, decision tree classifiers are widely recognized for their effectiveness as a supervised learning technique. Utilizing a divide-and-conquer approach, decision trees enable efficient data exploration and classification. Studies have demonstrated the application of decision tree algorithms to analyse historical performance data of engineering students. These models can predict student outcomes with significant accuracy, providing a mechanism to identify students at risk of failure. Such predictions empower educators to implement timely interventions, delivering targeted support and improving overall academic success. This approach underscores the potential of decision trees in transforming educational practices through data-driven insights.

Koutina and Kermanidis (2010) explored the importance of timely academic performance prediction for postgraduate students, particularly in MSc programs, where such insights are beneficial for tutors. Their research focused on identifying the most efficient machine learning techniques for predicting the final grades of postgraduate students in the Informatics department at Ionian University. The study utilized datasets from five academic courses, incorporating demographic information, in-term performance metrics, and in-class behavior features[38].To address challenges such as small dataset sizes and class value imbalances, the researchers employed techniques like resampling and feature selection—innovative approaches in performance prediction applications. Experiments with six classification algorithms revealed that Naïve Bayes and 1-NN achieved the best results, demonstrating higher accuracy compared to similar studies. This research highlights the potential of machine learning techniques to enhance the predictive accuracy of academic performance models, offering valuable insights for improving educational outcomes.

A study conducted by Nedeva and Pehlivanova (2021) to predict student performance and identify the key factors influencing academic outcomes. Their research underscores the importance of predictive models in enabling universities to identify at-risk students and implement timely interventions to improve educational results [39].The study evaluated the efficiency of four classification algorithms: BayesNet (BN), Multilayer Perceptron (MLP), Sequential Minimal Optimization (SMO), and Decision Tree (J48). The performance of these algorithms was compared using metrics such as True Positive Rate (TP Rate), Precision, F-Measure, Accuracy, and error measures (MAE, RMSE, RAE, and RRSE). The analysis was conducted using the Weka open-source software.Results revealed that the MLP algorithm outperformed the others, delivering the highest accuracy for the dataset used. Additionally, the study identified 12 attributes as the most significant factors impacting student performance. These findings demonstrate the potential of machine learning in creating effective predictive models, which can help universities enhance student outcomes through data-driven decision-making.

The primary aim of education has always been to improve quality, develop systems that provide strategic advantages to students, and predict academic success both during and after their academic tenure. Over the years, artificial intelligence (AI) and machine learning (ML) have emerged as transformative tools in this domain due to their capability to establish meaningful relationships and produce accurate predictions. These technologies have been extensively explored for predicting student performance and enhancing academic systems.Sekeroglu et al. (2020) conducted a systematic review of student performance prediction studies published between 2010 and 2020 across three major databases. Their analysis categorized the studies based on key components such as models, datasets, validation techniques, evaluation metrics, and research aims [40]. The review highlighted critical variations and gaps in the studies, such as inconsistent evaluation strategies and fragmented validation methods, which hinder the development of standardized practices in this field.Furthermore, the review emphasized that while various models have been explored, there is a growing need to adopt deep learning techniques for more precise predictions. The authors advocated for the establishment of global datasets facilitated by an international education information consortium, which could address several existing challenges. Such datasets would enhance the reproducibility of studies, provide comprehensive benchmarks, and facilitate collaboration across institutions.The findings from Sekeroglu et al. align with the broader academic consensus, emphasizing the necessity for standardization in methodologies and the adoption of advanced ML techniques. This review provides a foundational understanding of the trajectory of research in this area and underscores the importance of future studies focusing on scalable and globally applicable solutions.

Educational Data Mining (EDM) has emerged as a vital domain in enhancing the learning environment through advanced methods, techniques, and applications. The integration of machine learning (ML) and data mining techniques has provided tools to effectively explore and utilize educational data, aiding in the understanding of the student learning process. Modern academic institutions, operating within competitive and complex landscapes, face challenges in analysing student performance, delivering quality education, and devising strategies for evaluation and improvement [41].Albreiki et al. (2021) conducted a systematic review of EDM literature focusing on identifying student dropouts and predicting students at risk between 2009 and 2021. Their findings highlighted the widespread application of machine learning (ML) techniques to address these challenges. Two primary sources of data were identified in these studies: institutional databases from colleges and universities, and online learning platforms. The review confirmed the pivotal role of ML methods in predicting at-risk students and dropout rates, which in turn contributes to the development of targeted intervention plans aimed at improving student performance.The review underscored the necessity of implementing effective student intervention strategies to mitigate challenges faced by students during their academic journeys. By leveraging ML techniques, universities can proactively address risks, optimize learning outcomes, and enhance overall institutional performance. This body of research underscores the importance of EDM in addressing contemporary educational challenges and provides a foundation for future studies aimed at refining predictive models and intervention methodologies.

Student retention remains a critical challenge in higher education, requiring systematic approaches to identify at-risk students and address their needs effectively. Traditionally, managers and academics have relied heavily on intuition and personal experience to identify potential risk factors among students. However, these methods often lack the precision and early identification necessary for timely interventions [42].Gray and Perkins (2019) conducted an in-depth study examining the literature on learning analytics methods and measures. Their review highlighted the availability of tools aimed at addressing student retention; however, they noted a significant gap in the early identification of struggling students. In response, the authors proposed a novel approach involving the definition of a new descriptive statistic for student attendance. By applying advanced machine learning techniques, they developed a predictive model capable of identifying at-risk students as early as the third week of the fall semester, achieving approximately 97% accuracy.This predictive model was further contextualized within an appropriate pedagogical framework to ensure its integration into comprehensive student support mechanisms. The study emphasizes the importance of utilizing data-driven techniques like machine learning to enhance the precision and effectiveness of early intervention strategies. The findings underscore the potential of learning analytics to address challenges in student retention and contribute to the broader goal of improving educational outcomes in higher education.

In the evolving landscape of education, predicting students' academic performance has emerged as a significant area of research. Scholars such as Juan L. Rastrollo-Guerrero, Juan A. Gómez-Pulido, and Arturo Durán-Domínguez(2019) have contributed to this field, emphasizing the importance of leveraging technological advancements to enhance educational outcomes[43].The prediction of students' academic performance has become a crucial area of research in educational contexts, including schools and universities. This is primarily due to its potential to facilitate the design of effective mechanisms that enhance academic achievements and reduce dropout rates. The integration of technology-enhanced learning (TEL) systems has further augmented this field by automating many processes associated with students' activities. These systems generate and handle massive volumes of data, providing an opportunity to analyse and process information to extract meaningful insights into students' knowledge levels and their interactions with academic tasks.Analysing these data sources has become integral to developing predictive models and algorithms aimed at improving academic outcomes. Existing research highlights the role of Artificial Intelligence (AI) techniques in advancing this field. A detailed review of nearly 70 scholarly articles reveals that several modern AI-driven methodologies have been extensively employed to predict students' performance. Among these, Machine Learning (ML), Collaborative Filtering (CF), Recommender Systems (RS), and Artificial Neural Networks (ANNs) have emerged as the most prominent approaches.Machine Learning models are particularly noted for their ability to identify patterns and trends from historical data, enabling accurate predictions of student performance. Collaborative Filtering and Recommender Systems, originally designed for applications such as e-commerce, have been successfully adapted to educational settings to offer personalized learning recommendations. Additionally, Artificial Neural Networks have demonstrated a unique capability to process complex, non-linear relationships within large datasets, making them a powerful tool for performance prediction.The reviewed studies emphasize that these AI techniques not only enhance predictive accuracy but also support targeted educational interventions. By leveraging such methodologies, educators can identify at-risk students, personalize learning experiences, and optimize teaching strategies, thereby contributing to overall academic excellence. This literature review synthesizes the insights from existing research, presenting a comprehensive understanding of the methodologies employed and their implications for future studies in this domain.

The integration of machine learning techniques in the field of education has gained substantial attention due to its potential to predict students' academic performance and improve learning outcomes. According to Ofori, Maina, and Gitonga (2020), the application of machine learning algorithms provides a robust framework for early identification of students' performance trends, enabling timely interventions to enhance academic achievements. Their study, published in the Journal of Information and Technology, explores the role of predictive analytics in addressing critical educational challenges and guiding institutional policies [44].

Machine learning has proven effective in analysing large volumes of student data, facilitating accurate predictions of academic performance. These predictions are instrumental in identifying at-risk students, refining instructional practices, and providing constructive feedback to both educators and learners. However, Ofori et al. (2020) emphasize that the effectiveness of machine learning models varies based on the algorithms used and the contextual factors considered. Despite advancements, the lack of consensus on the best-performing machine learning model in education remains a notable gap in the literature.

The review highlights the influence of socioeconomic and demographic factors, such as family income, parental education levels, and employment status, on students' academic outcomes. These factors are often overlooked in the development and evaluation of machine learning models, leading to inconsistencies in prediction accuracy. Additionally, while many models focus on predicting performance, fewer studies address the application of machine learning in directly improving learning outcomes. This imbalance underscores the need for holistic approaches that integrate both predictive and outcome-improvement functionalities.

Furthermore, the study by Ofori et al. (2020) underscores the importance of accurately ranking machine learning models based on their prediction capabilities [45]. By identifying the most appropriate models for specific educational contexts, institutions can adopt data-driven strategies to enhance learning environments and improve graduation rates. The authors conclude that prioritizing predictive analytics in education is essential for fostering effective learning practices and institutional success.

This review consolidates existing research on the application of machine learning in education, identifying key challenges and future directions for improving both predictive accuracy and learning outcomes. The insights provided offer valuable guidance for researchers and practitioners seeking to harness the potential of machine learning in the academic domain. The application of machine learning techniques in the field of education has gained prominence due to its potential to analyse vast datasets and provide meaningful insights into students' academic performance. Tanuar, Heryadi, and Lukas (2018) conducted a study that explored the use of machine learning in predicting students' final year results (GPA) based on their first-semester performance [46]. Presented at the 1st 2018 INAPR International Conference, this study focuses on the use of data from computer science courses, comprising six subjects, one laboratory component, and the students' graduation year GPA.The researchers employed three machine learning techniques: Generalized Linear Model, Deep Learning, and Decision Tree. Their findings demonstrate the feasibility of predicting students' academic performance with considerable accuracy. Moreover, the study identifies the key factors influencing final-year performance, which could serve as a valuable resource for guiding students in their academic journey. These insights could enable educational institutions to implement early intervention strategies, equipping students to overcome potential challenges and improve their academic outcomes.

The study highlights the increasing importance of machine learning in the education sector, emphasizing its role in leveraging data to enhance decision-making processes. By analysing students' academic records and identifying patterns, machine learning provides actionable insights that can be utilized to design personalized learning paths and improve overall educational outcomes.This research underscores the potential of integrating machine learning techniques into the academic environment, offering a data-driven approach to predict performance and provide timely support to students. The study's contributions serve as a foundational reference for further exploration into the application of predictive analytics in education. The growing availability of educational data, particularly from technology-enhanced learning platforms, has opened new opportunities for analysing and improving students' learning experiences. Waheed et al. (2020) explore the potential of utilizing virtual learning environment (VLE) data to predict academic performance, leveraging deep learning models for accurate predictions. Their study, published in Computers in Human Behaviour, highlights how learning behaviour data, often captured through VLE clickstreams, can be used to identify at-risk students and initiate early intervention strategies [46]. This aligns with the broader trend in educational research, which emphasizes the role of data-driven decision-making in optimizing the learning process and outcomes.VLEs have become crucial tools for collecting and analysing data on students' interaction with course materials, which directly reflects their learning behaviours. According to Waheed et al. (2020), by applying a deep artificial neural network to VLE data, the study was able to predict student performance with an accuracy ranging from 84% to 93%. This performance significantly outperforms traditional models like logistic regression and support vector machines, which achieved accuracies of 79.82% to 85.60%

and 79.95% to 89.14%, respectively. These results underscore the advantage of deep learning models in capturing complex patterns within educational data, offering valuable insights into student engagement and performance. The study also emphasizes the importance of incorporating both legacy data and assessment-related data in the prediction models, a finding that is consistent with previous research. Students who accessed content from previous lectures, for instance, were found to demonstrate better academic performance. This reinforces the significance of engagement with course material over time, a factor that predictive models can effectively highlight.Waheed et al. (2020) argue that the application of deep learning to VLE data can not only help identify at-risk students but also guide higher education institutions in developing frameworks for pedagogical support. The study suggests that such data-driven models can assist in making informed decisions regarding educational strategies, ultimately contributing to the sustainability of educational systems. This body of work builds on existing literature that highlights the power of learning analytics and machine learning in the educational domain. It positions deep learning models as powerful tools for predicting academic performance and supporting decision-making processes aimed at improving educational outcomes.

Student placement has long been a critical challenge for educational institutions, especially in the context of engineering programs. With the increasing emphasis on globalization and international rankings, ensuring a high placement rate for students is essential not only for institutional reputation but also for their overall ranking on various national and international platforms. Maurya, Hussain, and Singh (2021) highlight the significance of student placement as a key factor influencing the success of educational institutions. They focus on utilizing machine learning models to predict the likelihood of a student's placement in the IT industry based on academic performance across several stages of their education.

The authors argue that factors such as the student's performance in class Tenth, Twelfth, and Graduation exams, as well as any backlogs in their graduation, play a crucial role in predicting their placement prospects. This aligns with the growing trend in educational research that seeks to utilize predictive analytics and machine learning techniques to address challenges in student placement and career guidance. Maurya et al. (2021) propose several supervised machine learning classifiers to analyse these factors, including Support Vector Machine (SVM), Gaussian Naive Bayes, K-Nearest Neighbour (K-NN), Random Forest, Decision Tree, Stochastic Gradient Descent (SGD), Logistic Regression, and Neural Networks [48].Through a comparative analysis of the classifiers, the authors examine the accuracy of the models using various parameters, including accuracy score, confusion matrix, Heatmap, and classification report. Key metrics such as precision, recall, F1-score, and support are used to evaluate the models' performance, offering a comprehensive assessment of each model's ability to predict placement outcomes. The results show varying levels of success across the classifiers, with all models tested on new data excluded from the original dataset to assess their generalizability and robustness.This study contributes to the growing body of literature that explores the application of machine learning techniques in educational settings, particularly in the area of student placement prediction. The use of these models can aid educational institutions in identifying at-risk students and offering timely interventions to improve placement outcomes. Furthermore, the findings of Maurya et al. (2021) underscore the need for more refined and customized predictive models to enhance decision-making processes and better support students in their academic and professional journeys.

The use of machine learning techniques for early identification of students requiring assistance has been a subject of research for several decades. Initially, the approaches were based on relatively static factors, such as students' educational background and responses to various questionnaires. However, recent studies have shifted towards leveraging dynamic data, such as students' progress on course assignments and their behaviour during lectures. This transition has been further enabled by advancements in technology, allowing continuous collection and analysis of educational data.Ahadi, Lister, Haapala, and Vihavainen (2020) explore the use of machine learning for detecting students who may need additional support early in their academic journey, specifically within the context of introductory programming courses [49]. The researchers focused on analysing students' source code snapshots—data accumulated throughout their programming process—using machine learning methods. Their findings demonstrated that it is possible to identify high- and low-performing students with high accuracy after just the first week of the course. This early detection allows for timely intervention by instructors, enabling them to offer targeted guidance to struggling students and provide more challenging assignments to high-performing individuals. The study further compares the performance of various machine learning techniques for predicting students' performance based on source code data, highlighting the effectiveness of their method in the context of an introductory programming course. Early identification of students' performance not only helps instructors provide tailored support but also allows for better monitoring of students who may pass despite struggling, ensuring they receive the necessary attention in subsequent courses.The findings underscore the importance of using real-time data from students' programming activities to enhance the learning experience, guiding instructors to deliver more personalized educational interventions and offering students the best chance for academic success.

The application of machine learning in educational contexts has gained significant traction due to the increasing volume and complexity of data within educational institutions. Researchers have consistently explored methodologies to extract actionable insights from educational datasets, aiming to enhance both student outcomes and instructional efficacy.

One notable approach is the integration of machine learning algorithms to develop predictive models for academic performance. Sokkhey and Okazaki (2020) investigated the efficacy of hybrid machine learning techniques in addressing the challenges of prediction accuracy [50]. Their work emphasized the utility of principal component analysis (PCA) combined with multiple machine learning algorithms, including random forest (RF), C5.0 decision tree (DT), naïve Bayes (NB), and support vector machines (SVM). The hybridization of PCA with these algorithms aimed to mitigate misclassification issues and optimize classification performance.

The study employed three distinct datasets to evaluate the robustness of the proposed models. The evaluation metrics included classification accuracy and root mean square error (RMSE), with a 10-fold cross-validation technique ensuring the reliability of the predictive outcomes. The results demonstrated that the hybrid models significantly outperformed traditional standalone machine learning approaches, delivering optimal classification and prediction results.

This work aligns with broader trends in educational data mining, where hybrid methodologies are increasingly recognized for their potential to enhance predictive performance. The incorporation of PCA as a pre-processing step highlights the importance of dimensionality reduction in improving algorithmic efficiency and accuracy. Furthermore, the use of multiple machine learning algorithms underscores the necessity of comparative analysis to identify the most effective approaches for specific datasets.

By addressing the challenges of misclassification and validating their approach across diverse datasets, the study contributes to the growing body of literature advocating for hybrid techniques in academic performance prediction. Future research could expand on these findings by exploring additional datasets or integrating other advanced machine learning methods to further enhance predictive accuracy.

The adoption of artificial intelligence (AI) and machine learning (ML) techniques has become increasingly prevalent in educational contexts, particularly in response to the disruptions caused by the COVID-19 pandemic. Various studies have demonstrated the potential of these technologies to address challenges related to remote learning, student performance prediction, and educational decision-making.

Ahajjam, Haidar, and Farhaoui (2021) proposed an AI-based recommendation system designed to predict student performance in Morocco's Guelmim Oued Noun region during the pandemic[51].The study highlighted the role of AI algorithms in facilitating decision-making processes traditionally performed by humans. By leveraging data science and machine learning techniques, the system aimed to provide actionable recommendations tailored to high school students' academic needs.

The study contextualized its approach within the broader shift to distance education prompted by the Moroccan Ministry of Education's suspension of in-person classes. This transition necessitated the development of alternative educational methods, including virtual counselling and guidance services. Central and regional administrative structures collaborated to ensure the continuity of educational services during this exceptional period, underscoring the need for innovative technological solutions.

The authors utilized data analysis and AI technologies to create a framework that addressed the challenges of remote learning. The inclusion of keywords such as "data science," "prediction," and "recommendation" reflects the study's focus on actionable insights derived from advanced computational models. By targeting high school students, the research emphasized the importance of personalized learning pathways in maintaining academic performance amidst unprecedented educational disruptions.

This study aligns with the growing body of literature emphasizing the transformative potential of AI and ML in education. The integration of these technologies into recommendation systems illustrates a practical application of predictive analytics, enhancing the ability to identify and address students' learning needs. Future research could build on these findings by expanding the scope to include a wider variety of datasets or exploring the long-term impacts of AI-based interventions on student outcomes.

Student engagement is widely recognized as a critical factor influencing academic performance. Engagement encompasses students' levels of passion, interest, and attention within educational environments, shaping their ability to achieve desired learning outcomes. Traditional learning systems often relied on direct interaction and active participation strategies, such as encouraging students to ask questions, take notes, and engage in discussions. Educators frequently employed these techniques to foster involvement and ensure that students remained attentive during instructional activities.

However, the rise of technology-enhanced learning systems (TELS) has transformed how engagement is cultivated and assessed in educational settings. Orji and Vassileva (2021) explored this paradigm shift by examining the relationship between student engagement and academic performance in an online learning environment. Their study focused on leveraging machine learning techniques to analyse activity logs from a TELS used in an undergraduate course. The activity logs, serving as objective and unbiased data, provided a comprehensive view of students' actual learning behaviour [52].

The authors employed both supervised (Random Forest) and unsupervised (Clustering) machine learning approaches to uncover patterns in the data. The results revealed a significant correlation between student engagement, assessment scores (derived from quizzes and assignments), and final academic performance. Engagement and assessment scores emerged as strong predictors of students' final grades, underscoring the importance of these factors in evaluating academic success.

This study highlights the potential of machine learning to provide actionable insights into student learning behaviours. By analysing objective data, researchers can identify patterns that might otherwise remain undetected in traditional evaluation methods. The findings also emphasize the need for data-driven interventions to enhance student engagement in online learning environments, addressing a critical gap in contemporary educational research.

The implications of these findings extend to the design of online learning systems, where adaptive strategies can be employed to increase engagement and, consequently, academic performance. Future research could expand on this work by exploring engagement predictors across diverse courses or integrating additional variables, such as social interactions and emotional engagement, to develop a more holistic understanding of the factors influencing student success.

The widespread adoption of social media among college and university students has sparked ongoing debates regarding its impact on academic performance. Social networking sites are frequently accessed both within and outside lecture halls, leading to questions about whether their usage hinders or enhances students' educational outcomes. Existing research on this topic presents divergent views, with some studies associating social media usage and multitasking with negative effects on academic performance, while others find little to no significant impact.

Nti, Akyeramfo-Sam, Bediako-Kyeremeh, and Agyemang (2021) sought to address these conflicting perspectives through a study examining the relationship between social media usage patterns and students' academic performance. Their research explored variables such as the rate and nature of social media use, usage during class sessions, and the level of exposure to social networking sites. The study utilized data from a sample of 550 students, collected through a convenience sampling method [53].

The authors employed machine learning algorithms, specifically Decision Tree (DT) and Random Forest (RF), to develop a predictive framework for evaluating the impact of social media usage on students' grade point averages (GPA). The findings revealed a partial effect, with certain aspects of social media usage, such as its frequency and in-class use, being moderately associated with variations in academic performance. These results suggest that while social media may not universally impede academic outcomes, specific patterns of use can influence performance to varying degrees.

This study contributes to the growing body of literature examining the interplay between technology use and educational outcomes. By applying machine learning techniques, the research provides a nuanced understanding of how social media behaviours relate to academic performance, addressing gaps in earlier studies that relied on traditional statistical methods. The inclusion of predictive analytics underscores the potential of data-driven approaches in identifying factors that may support or hinder student success.

Future research could expand on these findings by exploring longitudinal effects of social media usage on academic trajectories or examining its role in fostering collaborative learning and knowledge sharing. Additionally, incorporating qualitative methods could provide deeper insights into the motivations and contexts behind students' social media behaviours, offering a more comprehensive perspective on its educational implications.

Predicting student performance is a critical area of research in educational data mining, aiming to identify at-risk students and improve learning outcomes through timely interventions. Hasan and Rabby (2021) emphasised the importance of proactive strategies to support students in achieving better academic results by leveraging machine learning algorithms.

Their study focused on developing a system to predict students' future academic performance based on their current progress. This predictive model aimed to assist educators in identifying students who may struggle in upcoming examinations [54]. By analysing dependencies and patterns in students' academic data, the system provided actionable recommendations, such as course selection and targeted advice from teachers. The authors noted that such a system could address the challenge of personalised monitoring, which is often difficult for educators managing large groups of students.

The proposed machine learning model achieved a prediction accuracy of 94.88%, highlighting its effectiveness in identifying potential academic challenges. The research demonstrated that integrating artificial intelligence into educational processes could offer substantial benefits, including providing students with insights into their likely outcomes and personalized strategies to avoid poor performance. Teachers, in turn, could use the system to better understand individual student needs and offer tailored guidance.

This study aligns with broader efforts to integrate technology into education to enhance student support systems. By focusing on predictive analytics, the research contributes to a growing body of literature that explores how machine learning can be used to foster early intervention and improve academic success. The findings underscore the potential of data-driven tools to complement traditional teaching methods and address gaps in student advising and monitoring.

Future research could expand on these findings by exploring the scalability of such systems across diverse educational settings and student populations. Additionally, incorporating real-time feedback mechanisms or extending the model to include behavioural and demographic variables could provide a more holistic view of factors influencing academic performance.

Educational data mining (EDM) has become an essential tool for predictive analytics in the education sector, offering insights to guide decision-making and policy development. Olaleye and Vincent (2021) utilized EDM techniques to develop a predictive model for assessing the academic performance and risk levels of teachers-in-training at a College of Education in Nigeria [55].

The study focused on identifying key attributes from the academic data of graduate teachers and constructing a model to forecast their performance by categorizing their academic standing into risk levels. By analysing success indicators and assigning risk levels, the model provided school administrators with a valuable tool for monitoring and evaluating student performance. This proactive approach aimed to address academic challenges and enhance outcomes before graduation.

The findings revealed that core courses offered during the first and second semesters of the second year of study significantly influenced overall academic performance. Deficiencies in these courses increased the students' risk levels, underscoring the importance of early intervention in these critical areas. Interestingly, the study highlighted the relatively low impact of the teaching practice program—a six-month practical assignment—in predicting final academic standing. This observation suggests that while practical exposure is integral to teacher training, it may not be a strong determinant of academic success as measured by traditional evaluation metrics.

This research contributes to the growing body of literature on predictive modelling in education, emphasizing the importance of identifying high-impact academic indicators to support student achievement. By leveraging machine learning, the study highlights the potential for data-driven systems to improve educational outcomes and enable more effective resource allocation.

Future research could further explore the integration of non-academic factors, such as psychological or socio-economic variables, into predictive models to provide a more comprehensive understanding of risk factors. Additionally, extending the analysis to other educational contexts or institutions could validate the model's applicability across diverse learning environments.

Predicting student performance in higher educational institutions has become a critical focus in academic research, given its implications for resource management and student success in knowledge-based economies. Yakubu and Abubakar (2021) explored the use of machine learning techniques to predict academic outcomes based on early detection indicators such as age, gender, high school exam scores, region, and cumulative grade point average (CGPA).

The study utilized secondary data sourced from a Nigerian university's student information system to develop a predictive model. The findings revealed key insights into the factors influencing academic performance. Notably, age was found to have no significant correlation with academic success, as measured by CGPA. However, gender emerged as a predictive variable, with female students being 1.2 times more likely to achieve high CGPAs compared to their male counterparts. High entrance examination scores (e.g., JAMB scores) were positively associated with academic success, underscoring their predictive validity.

Regional disparities also played a role, with students from affluent and developed regions being more likely to achieve higher CGPAs, suggesting the influence of socio-economic factors on academic performance. Additionally, students in their third and fourth years of study were identified as more likely to excel academically, potentially due to increased academic maturity and specialization in their areas of study.

The predictive model presented by Yakubu and Abubakar offers significant utility as a classification tool for identifying at-risk students and implementing timely interventions. By promoting early detection and remediation, such models can help mitigate academic failures, enhance student outcomes, and optimize resource allocation in higher educational institutions [56].

This research contributes to the broader literature on machine learning applications in education, demonstrating how data-driven strategies can inform institutional policies and support student success. Future studies could expand the scope by incorporating additional variables, such as psychological or environmental factors, to create more comprehensive predictive models. Moreover, validating the model across diverse institutional settings would enhance its generalizability and applicability.

Predicting student academic performance is a critical area of focus for educational institutions as it facilitates informed decision-making and enhances student outcomes. Ha et al. (2021) conducted an empirical study exploring the application of machine learning techniques to predict the final Grade Point Average (GPA) of students based on a combination of personal characteristics, university entry scores, and academic progress during their first and second years of study.

The study utilized a dataset comprising survey responses from graduate students across three academic years and institutional data from a university's student management information system. The predictive variables included gender, living location, entry scores, gap years, and academic performance metrics from the first two years. By leveraging machine learning, the study examined the relationship between these factors and their influence on academic outcomes.

Key findings highlighted the correlation between the selected variables and student performance, affirming the impact of personal characteristics and prior academic achievements on final GPA. Notably, the study identified specific machine learning techniques as the most effective for predicting student performance, providing valuable insights into the appropriate methodologies for educational data analysis.

The research underscores the potential of machine learning in higher education, particularly in aiding faculty and administrators in making adjustments to curricula and teaching strategies based on predictive analytics. By enabling early identification of at-risk students, such predictive models can inform targeted interventions to enhance academic success.

This study contributes to the growing body of literature on the application of data-driven approaches in education. It provides a robust framework for integrating predictive analytics into institutional decision-making processes. Future research could expand upon this work by incorporating additional variables, such as socio-economic or psychological factors, to enhance the predictive accuracy of such models. Moreover, applying the findings across diverse educational contexts would validate the generalizability of the proposed techniques.

Predicting student performance has long been a central concern in education, with the potential to provide early interventions that can improve outcomes. In recent years, there has been a growing interest in leveraging deep learning techniques to address this challenge, as these methods can capture complex patterns and dynamics in student behaviour. Kim et al. (2021) introduced a novel approach for student performance prediction using deep learning, specifically through the GritNet model, which is based on the Bidirectional Long Short-Term Memory (BLSTM) architecture.

Traditional methods of predicting student performance, such as logistic regression, have shown some utility but often struggle with providing accurate early-stage predictions. Kim et al. (2021) approached the problem from a sequential event prediction perspective, recognizing that student performance is influenced by a series of events that unfold over time, especially in online learning environments. This perspective led to the development of GritNet, a deep learning algorithm designed to track and predict student outcomes as they interact with coursework on an online platform.

The study's results, based on real data from Udacity students, demonstrated that GritNet outperformed traditional logistic regression models, particularly in the first few weeks of a course, where predictions are most difficult due to the limited data available. GritNet's ability to capture temporal dependencies through the BLSTM architecture proved to be a significant advantage in forecasting student graduation probabilities, providing educators with a tool for early intervention in cases where students might need additional support.

This research contributes to the growing body of literature that explores the application of deep learning to educational data mining, offering a sophisticated approach to predicting student performance. The findings highlight the potential of deep learning to improve early-stage academic predictions, facilitating timely and targeted interventions. Future research could further refine these models by incorporating additional variables, such as social engagement or mental health factors, which could further enhance prediction accuracy and support proactive educational strategies.

This study adds to the literature by demonstrating how advanced machine learning techniques, specifically deep learning, can be effectively utilized to address complex educational challenges, offering significant potential for improving student success in online and traditional learning environments.

The field of precision education, which aims to tailor learning experiences to individual students' needs, has gained significant attention in recent years, driven by advancements in artificial intelligence (AI) and machine learning (ML) techniques. Luan and Tsai (2021) conducted a comprehensive review of 40 empirical studies that explore the application of machine learning in precision education. Their review provides a systematic analysis of how machine learning approaches are being employed to predict learning outcomes and identify students at risk of dropping out, with a particular focus on online and blended learning environments.

A common theme in the studies reviewed by Luan and Tsai (2021) is the use of machine learning for predicting student performance and dropout rates. These studies predominantly involved university students, particularly those studying computer science or STEM disciplines. The majority of the research employed data collected from various learning management systems (LMS), providing a rich source of behavioural and performance data for analysis. This aligns with the growing emphasis on data-driven strategies in education, which aim to identify patterns in student learning and intervene early to improve outcomes.

The review identified several machine learning algorithms commonly used in precision education, including decision trees, support vector machines (SVM), and neural networks. These algorithms are typically employed to analyse diverse sets of data, such as student demographics, learning behaviours, and academic performance, to make predictions about future outcomes. Evaluation methods and validation approaches varied across studies, with cross-validation being a popular technique for assessing model accuracy.

The authors also discussed emerging issues in the field, such as the challenges associated with data privacy and ethical considerations in using machine learning for educational purposes. Additionally, they identified areas for future research, including the need for more diverse datasets, the integration of more complex models, and the development of strategies to support personalized learning at scale.

Luan and Tsai's (2021) review contributes to the growing body of literature on machine learning in education, highlighting its potential for enhancing precision education. By providing insights into the current state of research, the paper encourages further exploration of how machine learning can be applied to predict and improve student learning outcomes, while also addressing the challenges and ethical considerations that come with the use of such technologies in educational settings.

This literature serves as a critical reference for researchers and educators interested in the integration of AI and machine learning into educational practices, providing a clear understanding of the current landscape and pointing towards future directions for development in precision education.

The application of machine learning algorithms in educational settings has been increasingly recognized as an effective tool for analysing various types of data, including student feedback. One notable area of exploration is the use of sentiment analysis to assess teacher performance based on student comments. Gutiérrez et al. (2018) examined this approach by developing a model called "Social Mining" to analyse student feedback and improve teaching techniques through the evaluation of teacher performance.

Sentiment analysis, a key technique in natural language processing, has gained widespread attention due to its success in understanding user preferences, behaviour patterns, and feedback, particularly in the realms of business and marketing. The application of sentiment analysis to education is a relatively recent but promising development aimed at enhancing the quality of teaching and learning environments. In the educational context, the analysis of student comments allows for the identification of strengths and weaknesses in teaching methods, which can lead to improved instructional strategies and more tailored educational experiences.

The Social Mining model developed by Gutiérrez et al. (2018) utilized machine learning algorithms, specifically Support Vector Machines (SVM) and Random Forest, to classify and analyse student comments regarding teacher performance. The model was implemented at the Universidad Polytechnic de Aguascalientes in Mexico, demonstrating its practical application in a higher education institution. The results indicated that sentiment analysis through machine learning algorithms could be highly effective in classifying teacher performance comments, achieving an impressive accuracy rate of 85%. This success highlights the potential of using sentiment analysis for teacher performance evaluation and its potential role in shaping future educational strategies.

The model's success further underscores the growing interest in using machine learning to enhance educational practices. It also emphasizes the need for robust evaluation metrics to assess the performance of machine learning algorithms in real-world educational contexts. As sentiment analysis continues to gain traction in education, future research may focus on refining these models to ensure greater accuracy, scalability, and adaptability to different educational environments.

In summary, the application of machine learning algorithms to analyse student feedback and assess teacher performance is a promising area of research that can significantly improve educational quality. Gutiérrez et al.'s (2018) work demonstrates the feasibility of using sentiment analysis to provide actionable insights into teaching methods, ultimately contributing to better learning experiences for students.

Chapter 3

Conceptual Framework

Student performance analysis using machine learning has several important benefits and can address various educational challenges. The key reasons for the need of student performance analysis in exams using machine learning is that Machine learning algorithms can analyze individual student performance data and tailor learning experiences to the specific needs and abilities of each student. This can help students learn at their own pace and be more engaged in their education.Machine learning (ML) can help in designing more effective exams and assessments by identifying questions or topics that are particularly challenging or not contributing significantly to student learning [1]. This tool can be used to conduct research and analysis in the field of education, enabling the discovery of new patterns, correlations, and trends in student performance data.

Institutions can use machine learning to ensure the quality and fairness of exams and assessments, minimizing bias and improving the assessment process.Providing insights into student performance to parents and students can foster greater engagement and motivation for improvement.

Student performance analysis using machine learning is crucial for enhancing the quality of education, improving student outcomes, and ensuring that educational institutions can adapt to the evolving needs of their students. It can be a powerful tool for educators, administrators, and policymakers to make data-driven decisions and support the success of students.

3.1 Statement of the problem

"Utilizing machine learning tools for student performance analysis in exams offers a transformative approach to education" [2].These tools empower educators, institutions, and policymakers to gain valuable insights from data, enabling personalized learning, early intervention, predictive analytics, and evidence-based decision-making. By harnessing the power of machine learning, we can better understand student strengths and weaknesses, adapt teaching strategies, and ensure that no student is left behind. This data-driven approach holds the potential to enhance educational outcomes, foster accountability, and create a more dynamic and responsive educational ecosystem.

3.2Objective of the study

The objective is to leverage Machine Learning techniques to predict student performance in exams, identify key factors influencing outcomes, and provide actionable insights for early interventions. This aims to enhance academic support, optimize learning strategies, and improve overall educational outcomes.

The objectives of student performance analysis in exams using machine learning are as follows:

3.2.1 Enhancing Student Outcomes: To identify at-risk students and predict academic trends, enabling timely interventions and proactive measures to improve student performance and retention.

3.2.2 Optimizing Educational Resources: To provide data-driven insights for refining curricula, teaching strategies, and resource allocation, ensuring alignment with student needs and institutional goals.

3.2.3 Promoting Data-Driven Decision-Making: To empower educators and policymakers with transparent and objective analyses for informed decisions, fostering accountability, continuous improvement, and equitable education.

The ultimate goal of student performance analysis using machine learning is to enhance the quality of education, improve student outcomes, and ensure that educational institutions are equipped to adapt and respond to the evolving needs of their students [3]. It enables data-driven decision-making, fosters transparency, and helps create a more effective and equitable educational environment.

3.3. Scope of work:

The scope involves using Machine Learning models to predict student performance in examinations by analysing academic, behavioural, and demographic data. This includes:-

3.3.1. Data Collection: Gathering various types of data such as gender, race/ethnicity, parental education, test preparation course, math, reading, reading and writing etc. Data can be collected from various sources like learning management systems, surveys, and historical academic records.

3.3.2. Data Pre-processing: Cleaning and pre-processing the collected data to remove noise and inconsistencies. Handling missing data and outliers.

3.3.3. Feature Selection/Extraction: Identifying relevant features that can influence student performance. Extracting meaningful features from the data.

3.3.4. Model Development: Employing supervised learning technique using linear regression. In Supervised learning technique, the training data provided to the machines work as the supervisor that teaches the machines to predict the output correctly [4]. It applies the same concept as a student learns in the supervision of the teacher. The aim of a supervised learning algorithm is to find a mapping function to map the input variable(x) with the output variable(y).Linear regression is a type of supervised machine learning algorithm that computes the linear relationship between the dependent variable and one or more independent features by fitting a linear equation to observed data.

3.3.5. Model Evaluation: Assessing the performance of the model using appropriate metrics. The cross-validation and hyper parameter tuning to ensure the robustness of the model.

3.3.6. Visualisations and Interpretation: Visualizing the results with the help of powerful library module of python mainly **matplotlib** and **seaborn** for easy interpretation. With the help of Visualisations understanding the factors that influence student performance [5].

3.3.7. Integration with present educational systems to give the industrial use of the project: The scope of the proposed system "Student's Performance Analysis in Examination" is to integrate the developed models with existing educational system which will help the teachers and the educators to better analyse the student's performance and work in proper direction for the betterment in the child development [6]. As we know in modern way of teaching and learning methodology in schools and colleges teachers and educators keep the records of all kind of performance of the students and on the basis of their performance their further training and teaching methodology works. As we know that if in a class there are 30 students and each and every student have their own level of learning capabilities and different level of potential from the very childhood. This type of implementation of performance is done in international school of India and in abroad. This work of implementation will be shown in my thesis.

3.3.8. Privacy and Ethics: The work will ensure the privacy and security of student data.

3.4 Hypothesis

Analyzing factors that influence student performance is a complex and multifaceted task, often conducted in the field of education and psychology. The hypothesis is a fundamental part of this analysis, as it provides a testable statement about the relationships between different variables. Here are some common factors that researchers might investigate in their analysis of student performance, along with potential hypotheses for each factor: The research hypotheses are based on theoretical reasoning and results from previous studies, as explained in the literature survey section of this study. Given these considerations, we formed the following hypotheses whose work will be proved in my thesis.

3.4.1. Hypothesis 1: The performance of the students is better if the parents have a better level of education. This hypothesis I will be prove in my further research work with the findings because we know that the education of the parents impact the performance of the students in examination.

3.4.2. Hypothesis 2: In checking the performance of test course which is divided in math, reading and writing score. We know both the gender male and female have almost same IQ level but to many other different research and observation we come to know that that male have better reasoning power than the female. This hypothesis will be shown in my further research with my findings.

3.5. Delimitation of the Study

Delimitations of student performance analysis in exams using machine learning refer to the boundaries, restrictions, or limitations of this approach. It's essential to understand these limitations to make informed decisions and interpretations. Here are some common delimitations:

3.5.1. Availability of Data: Not all educational institutions may have access to comprehensive historical data, which is essential for creating effective machine learning models.

3.5.2. Generalizability: Machine learning models developed for one educational context or demographic might not be directly transferable to others. The effectiveness of a model can vary across different settings and student populations.

3.5.3. Interpretable Models: Many machine learning models, such as deep learning neural networks, are often considered black-box models, making it challenging to interpret why a particular prediction was made. This lack of interpretability can be a limitation in educational settings where explanations are required.

3.5.4. Resource Constraints: The implementation of machine learning in education may require significant resources, including computational power, software development, and expertise. Smaller educational institutions or less affluent regions may face constraints in this regard.

3.5.5. **Human Factors:** Machine learning models can't replace the human element in education. Teachers, counselors, and administrators play critical roles in providing guidance, motivation, and support to students.

3.5.6. **Overreliance on Data:** There's a risk that educators and institutions might overly on machine learning predictions, potentially neglecting the holistic development of students.

3.5.7. **Inherent Uncertainty:** Machine learning predictions are probabilistic, not deterministic. There's always an element of uncertainty in the predictions, which can make decisions based on these predictions challenging.

It's crucial to recognize these delimitations when implementing machine learning in education to make the most of its potential while being aware of its constraints and ethical considerations.

Chapter 4

Plan and Procedure of the Study

The research methodology used in my research is the experimental approach. Experimental research methodology is a scientific approach used to investigate causal relationships between variables by manipulating one or more independent variables and observing the effect on dependent variables. It is a cornerstone of the scientific method and is commonly used in fields like psychology, medicine, social sciences, educational field and natural sciences. Experimental research methodology is a powerful tool for testing hypotheses and uncovering causal relationships. Its rigorous approach and structured design make it invaluable in many scientific disciplines. By carefully planning and executing experiments, researchers can obtain reliable and valid results that contribute significantly to knowledge and practice.

Analysing student performance in examinations using machine learning is an insightful approach to understand various factors that contribute to academic success [7]. Here's an outline of an experimental approach being considered in my study:

4.1 Statement of Research Problem

Despite advancements in educational strategies and resources, a significant number of students continue to underperform in exams. This underperformance can be attributed to factors including socio-economic background, psychological conditions, study habits, and instructional methods. Traditional approaches to identifying and assisting at-risk students often lack the precision and timeliness needed to be effective. This research seeks to address this issue by leveraging machine learning (ML) techniques to predict student performance and recommend personalized interventions.

In the realm of education, understanding the multifaceted determinants of student performance in examinations is pivotal for devising effective interventions to enhance learning outcomes. This study aims to leverage machine learning techniques to comprehensively analyse the diverse array of factors influencing student performance in examinations. By delving into datasets encompassing student demographics, academic history, socio-economic background, and test preparation course and other affecting factors too[8].This research endeavors to develop predictive models capable of discerning patterns and elucidating key predictors of academic success.

4.2. Research Design

The research design which will be used in my research work to analyse the student's performance in examination will be experimental design in which one or more independent variables like parental level of education, race/ethnicity, gender and lunch is used to observe their effect on a dependent variable like test preparation course completed or not and math, reading and writing score. It allows to establish cause-and-effect relationships between variables. Experimental research design is a framework of protocols and procedures created to conduct experimental research with a scientific approach using two sets of variables. Experimental research helps to gather the necessary data for making better research decisions and determining the facts of a research study. A researcher can conduct experimental research when time is an important factor in establishing a relationship between the cause and effect. When there is an invariable or never-changing behaviour between the cause and effect. When the researcher wishes to understand the importance of the cause and effect. To publish significant results, choosing a quality research design forms the foundation to build the research study. Moreover, effective research design helps establish quality decision-making procedures, structures the research to lead to easier data analysis, and addresses the main research question. Therefore, it is essential to cater undivided attention and time to create an experimental research design before beginning the practical experiment. By creating a research design, a researcher is also giving oneself time to organize the research, set up relevant boundaries for the study, and increase the reliability of the results. Through all these efforts, one could also avoid inconclusive results. If any part of the research design is flawed, it will reflect on the quality of the results derived. A research study could conduct pre-experimental research design when a group or many groups are under observation after implementing factors of cause and effect of the research. The pre-experimental design will help researchers understand whether further investigation is necessary for the groups under observation [9]. Experimental research is often the final form of a study conducted in the research process which is considered to provide conclusive and specific results. But it is not meant for every research. It involves a lot of resources, time, and money and is not easy to conduct, unless a foundation of research is built. Yet it is widely used in research institutes and commercial industries, for its most conclusive results in the scientific approach.

4.3.Sampling design:

We will be using random sampling technique to collect student's data such as gender, race/ethnicity, parental level of education, lunch, test preparation course, math score, reading score and writing score which are the affecting factors for the analysis of student performance. Random sampling is a technique used to select a subset of individuals from a larger population in such a way that every individual has an equal chance of being chosen. When applied to studying student performance in examinations, random sampling ensures that the results are representative of the entire student population. To apply random sampling to study student performance firstly identifying the group of students we want to study. This could be all students in a particular school, grade, class, or a larger educational district. Then determining the sample size. After that decision on the number of students you need to sample here we have taken the record of 1000 students. Simple random sampling is done in which a random number generator is used to select unique numbers. These numbers correspond to the students' ID numbers. The sample size depends on the desired level of accuracy and the population size. Statistical formulas or sample size calculators can help determine this. The assurance of the data collection process is standardized to maintain consistency. Using statistical methods to analyse the performance data. Calculate averages, variances, and other relevant metrics.

4.4. Tools & Techniques

In research, tools and techniques serve various purposes, aiding in data collection, analysis, visualization, and interpretation. Analysing student performance in exams involves a variety of tools and techniques. Machine learning projects involve several stages, from data collection and pre-processing to model development, evaluation, and deployment [10]. Here are the key tools and techniques commonly used in my research in each stage:

Data Collection- Data collection for machine learning involves gathering labelled or unlabelled data from various sources to train, validate, and test models, ensuring they learn patterns effectively for accurate predictions.

Tools for Data collection: There are many tools and libraries available for machine learning, catering to a variety of tasks such as data pre-processing, model training, evaluation, and deployment. Here are some widely used tools for machine learning:

• **Data Repositories:** We have been using secondary data in form of datasets from Kaggle for machine learning which offers several benefits like diverse range of datasets, high-quality data, large dataset repository, data exploration, visualization and educational resources. Kaggle is a great resource for finding datasets related to student performance analysis.[11]. We have taken the datasets of students of 1000 records which is csv file (Excel format).These dataset contains information about student performance in secondary education, including demographic data, social factors, and academic performance.

Techniques:

• **Database Queries:** Retrieving data from relational and non-relational databases. SQL is a short-form of the structured query language, and it is pronounced as S-Q-L or sometimes as See-Quell. This database language is mainly designed for maintaining the data in relational database management systems. It is a special tool used by data professionals for handling structured data (data which is stored in the form of tables). It is also designed for stream processing in RDMS (Relational Database Management System). You can easily create and manipulate the database, access and modify the table rows and columns, etc. The basic use of SQL for data professionals and SQL users is to insert, update, and delete the data from the relational database. SQL allows the data professionals and users to retrieve the data from the relational database management systems. It also helps them to describe the structured data. It allows SQL users to create, drop, and manipulate the database and its tables. It also helps in creating the view, stored procedure, and functions in the relational database. It allows you to define the data and modify that stored data in the relational database. It also allows SQL users to set the permissions or constraints on table columns, views, and stored procedures.

- **IDE(Integrated Development Environment For Programming)** –

Anaconda 3 Navigator offers several benefits for machine learning (ML) practitioners especially for package management, pre-installed libraries, cross-platform compatibility, virtual environments and community support. Anaconda includes popular IDEs like Jupyter Notebook, which provide powerful tools for developing, debugging, and visualizing machine learning models.

- **Platform: Jupyter Notebook for Python Programming (Version 6.3.0):**

Jupyter Notebook is a widely used interactive computing environment that allows users to create and share documents containing live code, equations, visualizations, and narrative text. Jupyter Notebook, particularly version 6.3.0, is beneficial for machine learning programming. Some of the interactive features of Jupyter Notebook are interactive development, visualization, documentation, code reusability, experimentation & prototyping, integration with data analysing tools.

- **Computer programming in Python Version 3**

Python 3 is particularly useful for machine learning programming due to its rich ecosystem, ease of use, community support, flexibility and easy integration as python seamlessly integrates with other technologies commonly used in machine learning workflows, such as data manipulation libraries. Overall, Python's combination of simplicity, versatility, and powerful libraries makes it an ideal choice for machine learning programming [12].

4.5. Data Pre-processing

Data pre-processing is a crucial step in any machine learning project, as it ensures that the data is clean, consistent, and suitable for modelling. When analysing student performance, you'll typically deal with various types of data, such as numerical scores, categorical variables (e.g., gender, class), and potentially missing values.

4.6. Flow chart

A **flowchart** is a diagram that visually represents the steps, decisions, and processes in a system or program. It uses specific symbols to illustrate the flow of operations, making it easier to understand complex logic or workflows.

The work flow (Flow Chart) of the Program:

Fig 4.1: Flow chart of the Program

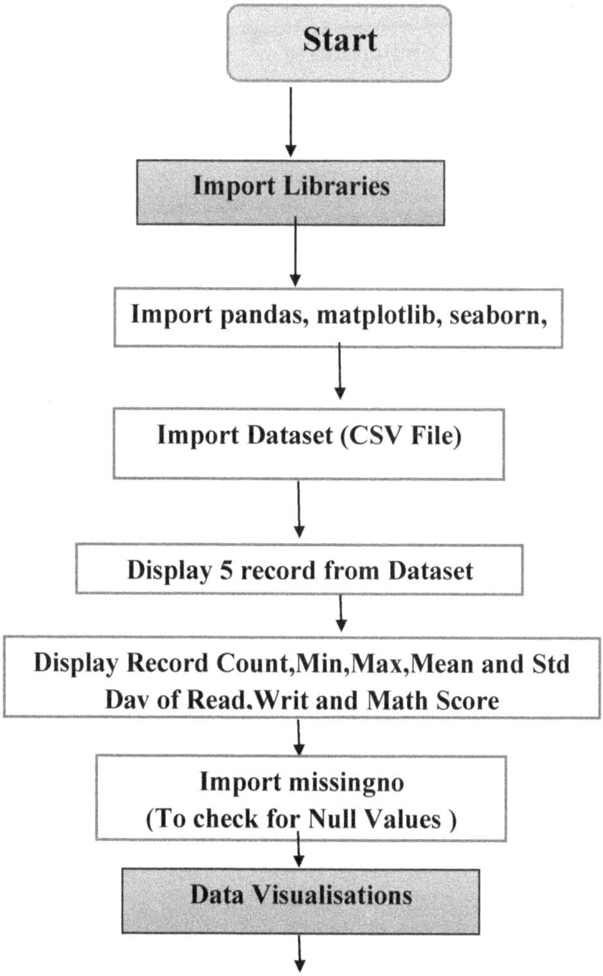

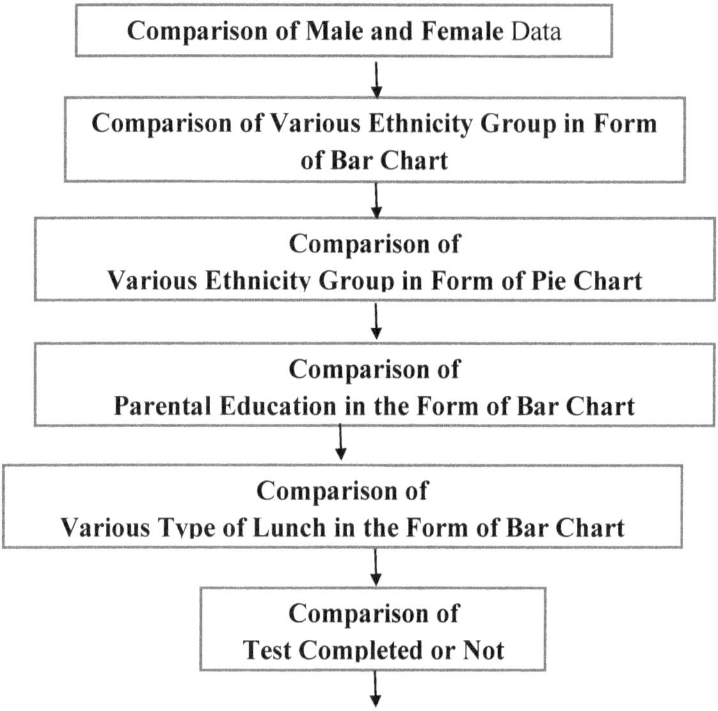
Comparison of Male and Female Data
Comparison of Various Ethnicity Group in Form of Bar Chart
Comparison of Various Ethnicity Group in Form of Pie Chart
Comparison of Parental Education in the Form of Bar Chart
Comparison of Various Type of Lunch in the Form of Bar Chart
Comparison of Test Completed or Not

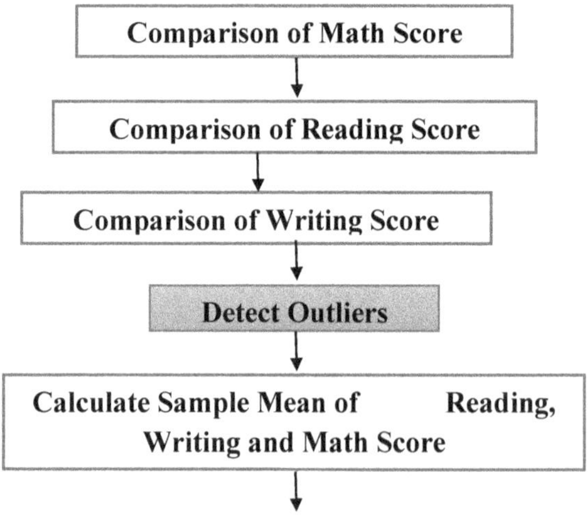
Comparison of Math Score
Comparison of Reading Score
Comparison of Writing Score
Detect Outliers
Calculate Sample Mean of Reading, Writing and Math Score

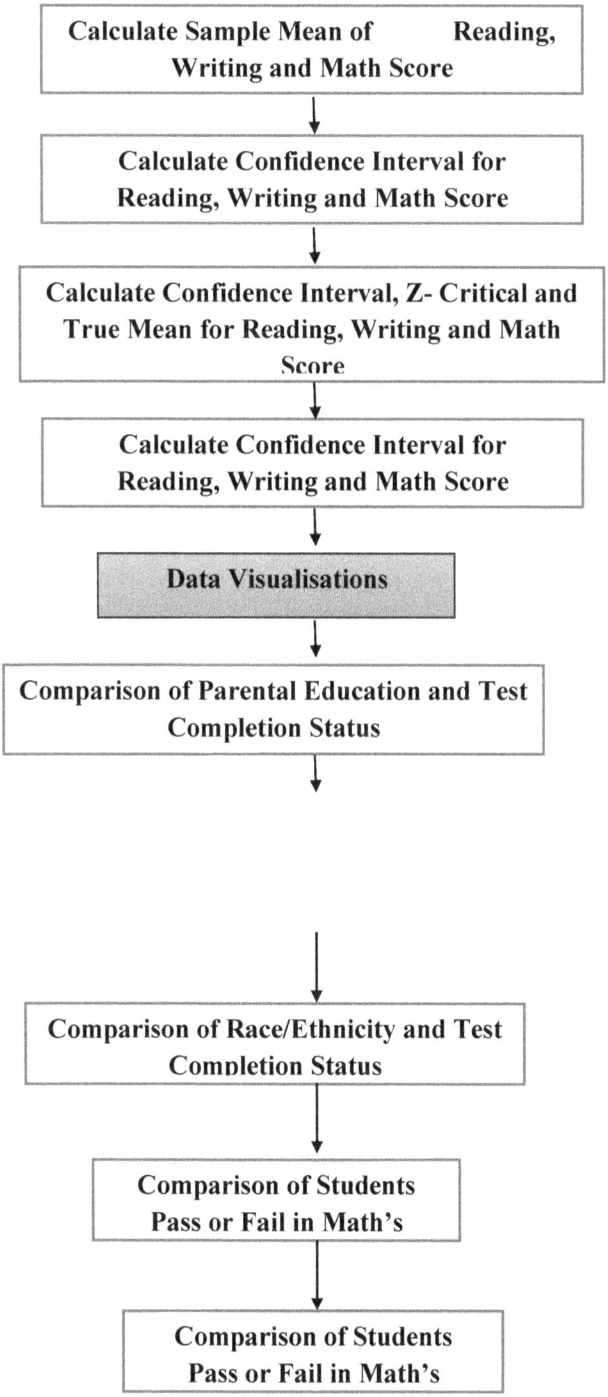
Calculate Sample Mean of Reading, Writing and Math Score
Calculate Confidence Interval for Reading, Writing and Math Score
Calculate Confidence Interval, Z- Critical and True Mean for Reading, Writing and Math Score
Calculate Confidence Interval for Reading, Writing and Math Score
Data Visualisations
Comparison of Parental Education and Test Completion Status
Comparison of Race/Ethnicity and Test Completion Status
Comparison of Students Pass or Fail in Math's
Comparison of Students Pass or Fail in Math's

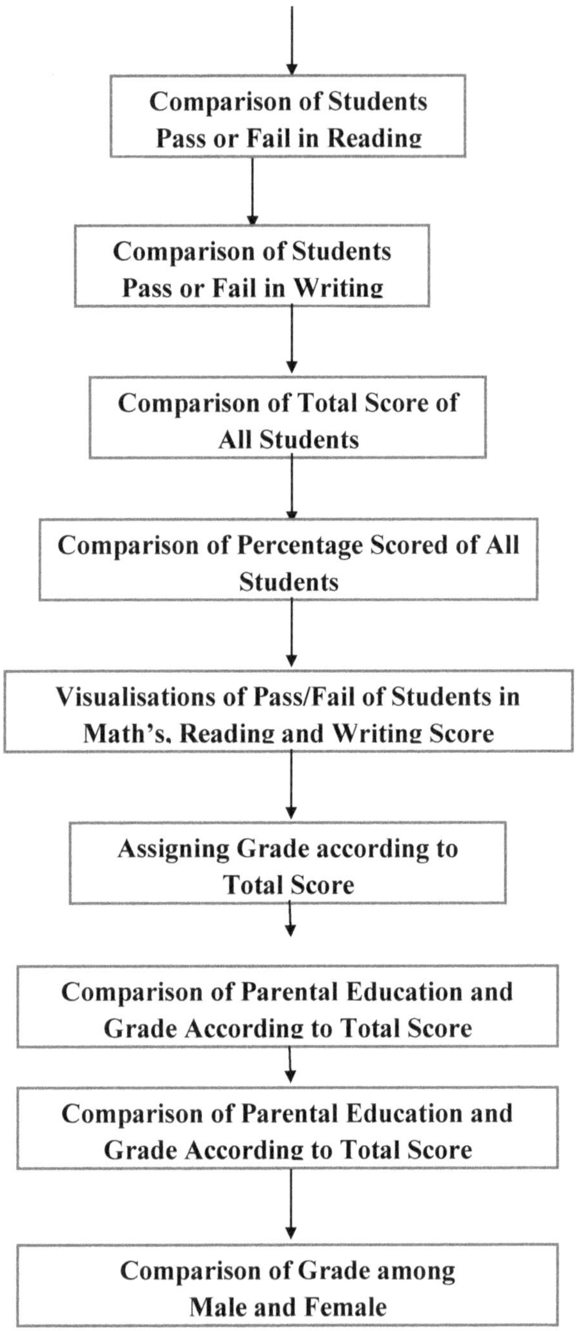
Comparison of Students Pass or Fail in Reading
Comparison of Students Pass or Fail in Writing
Comparison of Total Score of All Students
Comparison of Percentage Scored of All Students
Visualisations of Pass/Fail of Students in Math's, Reading and Writing Score
Assigning Grade according to Total Score
Comparison of Parental Education and Grade According to Total Score
Comparison of Parental Education and Grade According to Total Score
Comparison of Grade among Male and Female

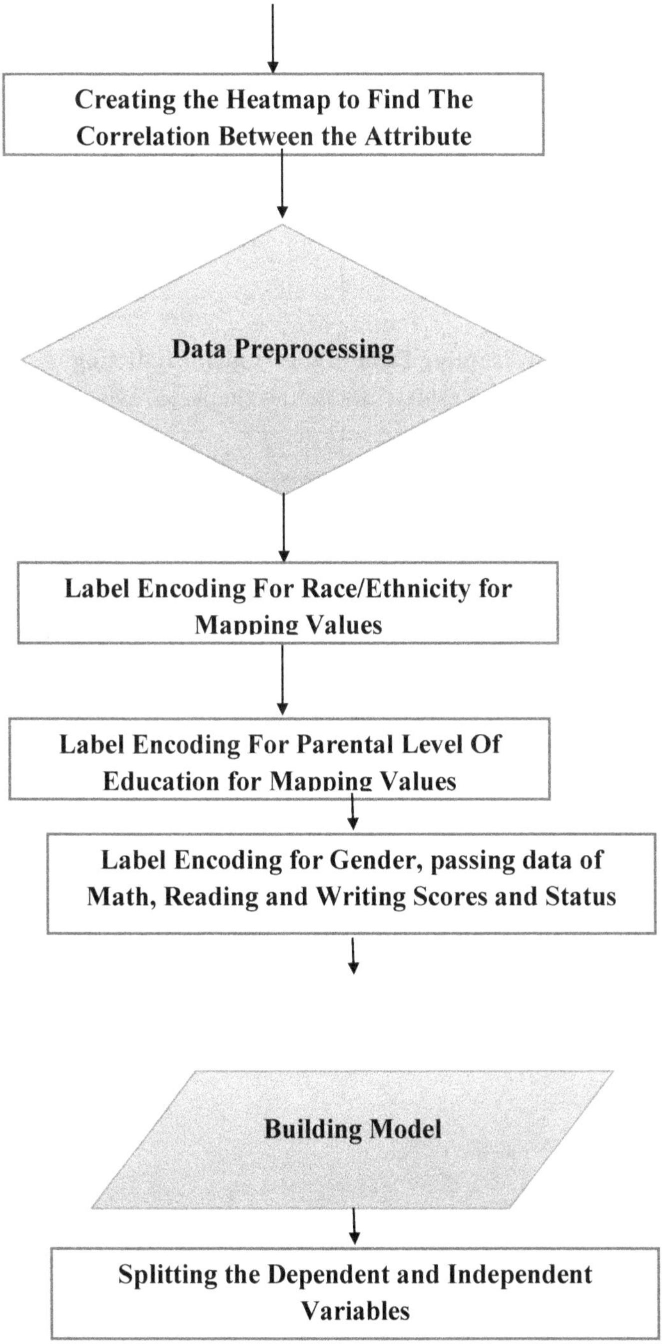
Creating the Heatmap to Find The Correlation Between the Attribute
Data Preprocessing
Label Encoding For Race/Ethnicity for Mapping Values
Label Encoding For Parental Level Of Education for Mapping Values
Label Encoding for Gender, passing data of Math, Reading and Writing Scores and Status
Building Model
Splitting the Dependent and Independent Variables

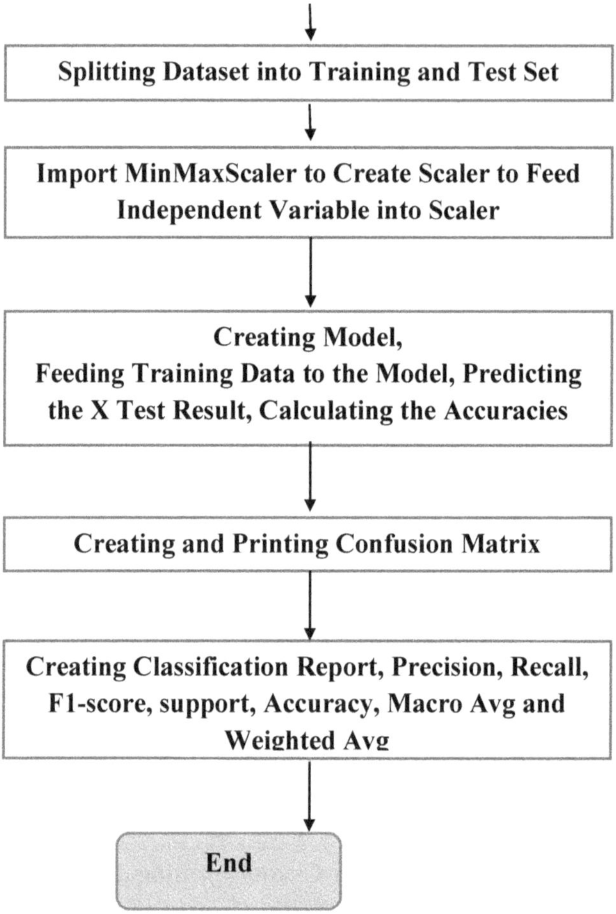

Importing libraries & datasets

```
6/12/22, 7:08 PM                                StudentPerformanceAnalysis - Jupyter Notebook

In [2]:

#import basic libraries and load the dataset

In [2]:

# for visualizations
import pandas as pd
import numpy as np
import matplotlib.pyplot as plt
import seaborn as sns
%matplotlib inline
sns.set_style("whitegrid")
plt.style.use("fivethirtyeight")
```

Fig 4.2: Python Code to Import Libraries for performing machine learning and loading dataset

Importing Libraries

Python offers a wide range of libraries for various purposes, from data analysis and machine learning to web development and database interaction. Some of the most popular Python libraries for my work is:

Pandas- To work with data in the form of table, data frame we need to import pandas library that provides high-performance data manipulation in Python. Pandas Data Frame is a widely used data structure which works with a two-dimensional array with labelled axes (rows and columns).

NumPy- NumPy provides a convenient and efficient way to handle the vast amount of data. Numpy is also very convenient with Matrix multiplication and data reshaping [13]. Numpy is fast which makes it reasonable to work with a large set of data.

Matplotlib: Matplotlib is a Python library which is defined as a multi-platform data visualization library built on Numpy array.

Seaborn: Seaborn is one of library for visualization of the graphical statistical plotting in Python. Seaborn provides many colour palettes and defaults styles to make the creation of many statistical plots in Python.

CODE EXPLAINATION

#import basic libraries and load the dataset

 # for visualizations

import pandas as pd

Explanation: import pandas libraries as pd as the variable

import numpy as np

Explanation: import numpy libraries as np as the variable

import matplotlib.pyplot as plt

Explanation: pyplot is a state-based interface to matplotlib. It provides an implicit, MATLAB-like, way of plotting. The above code import matplotlib libraries as plt as the variable

import seaborn as sns

Explanation: import seaborn libraries as sns as the variable

%matplotlib inline

Explanation: %matplotlib widget and inline are commands enables interactive plots in a widget-based window.

```
sns.set_style ("whitegrid")

plt.style.use ("fivethirtyeight")
```

4.7. Data Cleaning

Data cleaning is a crucial step in the data analysis process to ensure the quality and integrity of the data. Python offers a variety of tools and libraries that make data cleaning more efficient and effective. Here are some key tools and techniques:

Data cleaning through pandas helps in data manipulation and analysis. It provides data structures like Data Frame and Series which are very useful for cleaning and transforming data. **Common tasks with Pandas is h**andling missing data, removing duplicates, transforming data formats, filtering data and combining datasets[14].

NumPy is used for working with arrays and provides a high-performance multidimensional array object and tools for working with these arrays. **Common tasks with NumPy** is handling missing data, array operations and .statistical operations. Using these tools and techniques, we can effectively clean and pre-process your data, making it ready for analysis. Each tool has its strengths, and often a combination of these will be required to achieve the best results.

```
In [3]:

data = pd.read_csv('StudentsPerformance.csv')

In [4]:

data.head()

Out[4]:
```

	gender	race/ethnicity	parental level of education	lunch	test preparation course	math score	reading score	writing score
0	female	group B	bachelor's degree	standard	none	72	72	74
1	female	group C	some college	standard	completed	69	90	88
2	female	group B	master's degree	standard	none	90	95	93
3	male	group A	associate's degree	free/reduced	none	47	57	44
4	male	group C	some college	standard	none	76	78	75

Table 4.1. Code to read dataset and displaying some of the data

data = pd.read_csv ('StudentsPerformance.csv')

Explanation: StudentPerformance.csv is a excel file which store 1000 records using pd.read_csv() function

data = pd.read_csv ('StudentPerformance.csv')

This code is used to import StudentPerformance.csv (Excel File) which is approximately 1000 records.

This StudentPerformance.csv contains following data records.

Gender, race/ethnicity, parental level of education, lunch, test preparation course, maths score, reading score, writing score.

data.head()

This is a method in Pandas that is used to display the first few rows of a Dataframe. It's particularly useful for quickly inspecting the structure and contents of the Dataframe, especially when dealing with large datasets. Here's how you can use data.head():

Ensure that the data is well-organized, properly labelled, and free from errors or inconsistencies.

Using data.info()

This code is used in Python with a pandas Dataframe that can provide valuable insights into the structure and types of data present, which is essential for student performance analysis in exams using machine learning.

data.info()

Here's how data.info() can help in student performance analysis:

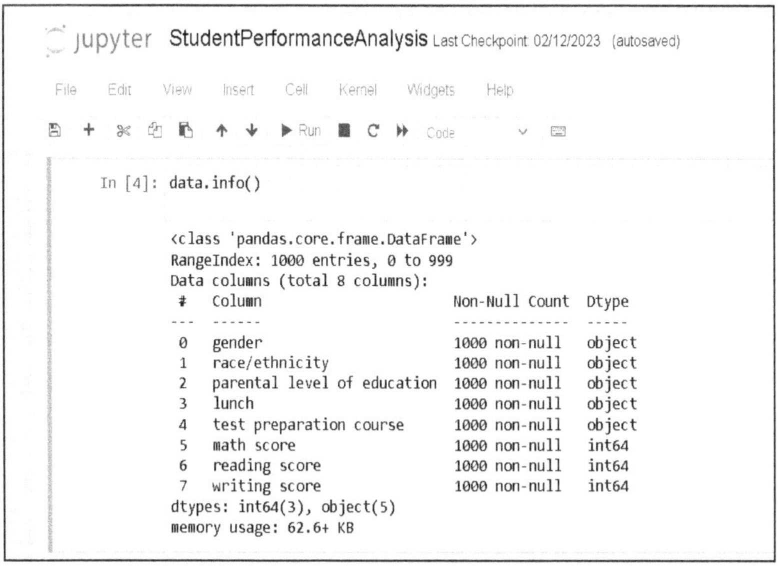

Table 4.2: Code to display Non Null Values

Data Types: data.info() will display the data types of each column. This is crucial because it helps identify numerical features (e.g., exam scores, study time) and categorical features (e.g., gender, education level).

Missing Values: data.info() will show the number of non-null values in each column. This allows you to identify if there are any missing values in the dataset, which might require handling before applying machine learning algorithms.

Memory Usage: data.info() also provides information about the memory usage of the Data Frame. While not directly related to student performance analysis, it's useful for understanding the memory footprint of your dataset, especially if dealing with large datasets.

Once we have a clear understanding of the structure and types of data present in your dataset using data.info(), you can proceed with various machine learning tasks such as data pre-processing, feature engineering, model training, and evaluation to analyse student performance in exams.

- For descriptive Statistics we use this command

  Data.describe().T

  Using Data.describe().T in the context of student performance analysis in examswith machine learning can provide a concise summary of the statisticalproperties of the dataset's numerical features.

  It provides information about the central tendency of numerical features, including mean and median. This can help you understand the average performance of students in exams.

  Spread of Data: Summary statistics like standard deviation, minimum, andmaximum values give insights into the spread of data. For example, a largestandard deviation might indicate a wide variation in student performance.

Quartiles: The quartiles (25th, 50th, and 75th percentiles) provide informationabout the distribution of data. This can be useful for identifying any skewness oroutliers in the performance data.

Count: The count column indicates the number of non-null values for eachnumerical feature. This helps in identifying missing values, which may need tobe handled before applying machine learning algorithms.

By examining the summary statistics generated by **Data.describe().T**, **W**e cangain valuable insights into the distribution and characteristics of

Numericalfeatures in the student performance dataset [15]. This understandingcan guide further analysis and pre-processing steps before applying machinelearningalgorithms for student performance prediction or analysis.

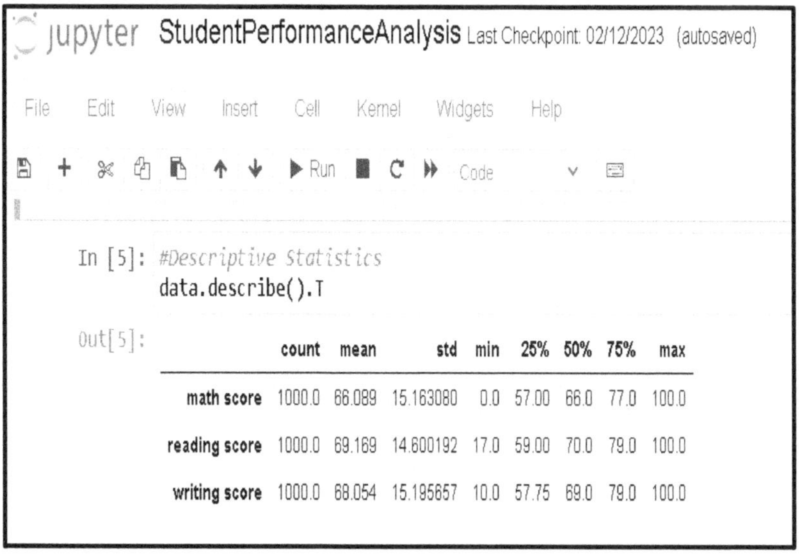


```
#Descriptive Statistics
data.describe().T
```

	count	mean	std	min	25%	50%	75%	max
math score	1000.0	66.089	15.163080	0.0	57.00	66.0	77.0	100.0
reading score	1000.0	69.169	14.600192	17.0	59.00	70.0	79.0	100.0
writing score	1000.0	68.054	15.195657	10.0	57.75	69.0	79.0	100.0

Table 4.3: Code to show the count, mean, Standard Deviation, Min value, 25%, 50%, 75% value and max value of math, reading and writing score

- Use !pip install missingno

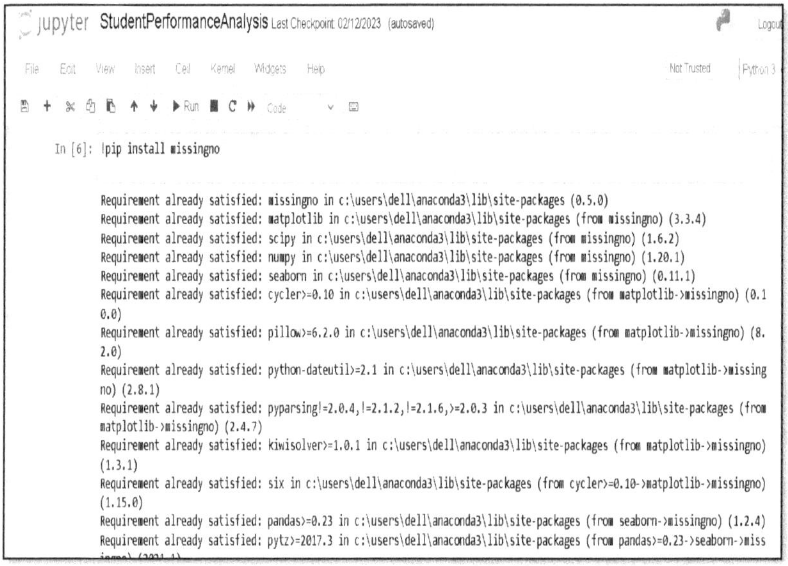

Fig 4.3. Code to import missingno library for visualising missing data in a dataset

The missingno library is useful for visualizing missing data in a dataset, which can be crucial in student performance analysis using machine learning. We can install and use missingno in analysis:

Once you've installed missingno, you can use it to visualize missing data in your student performance dataset like so:

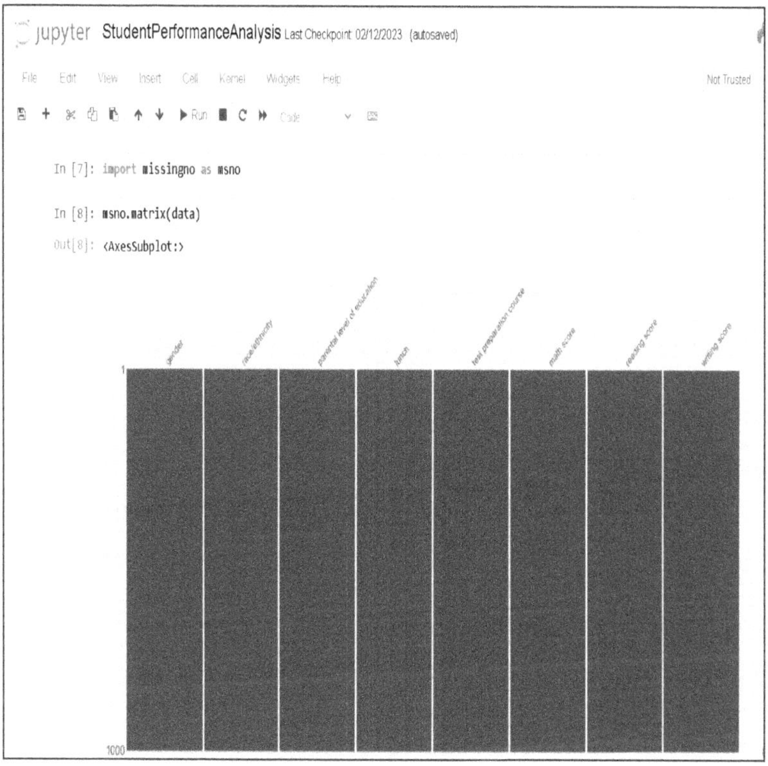

Fig. 4.4: Output to display Non Null values of all column

- Use of importing **missingno as msno**

Importing missingno as msno is a common convention and makes it easier to reference the library in your code. We import missingno as msno and use it for visualizing missing data in student performance analysis:

The visualization produced by msno.matrix() will help to identify missing data patterns in your student performance dataset, aiding in data pre-processing and ensuring the quality of your dataset for machine learning analysis [16].

4.8. Data Visualization

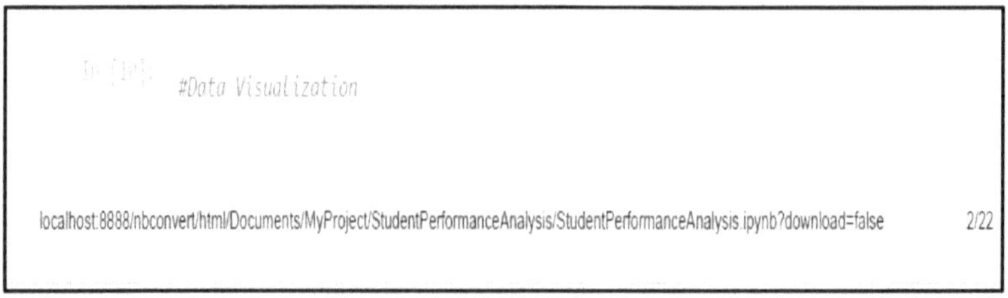

Fig. 4.5: Comment to show the code for Data Visualisation

Data visualization is crucial in student performance analysis as it allows you to explore patterns, trends, and relationships within the data. Here are some common types of visualizations that can be useful in student performance analysis using machine learning:

Histograms: Histograms can be used to visualize the distribution of exam scores or other numerical variables. They provide insights into the spread and shape of the data, helping to identify any patterns or anomalies.

Bar Charts: Bar charts can be used to compare the performance of different groups of students based on categorical variables such as gender, ethnicity, or education level. They can also be used to compare average scores across different exams or subjects.

Scatter Plots: Scatter plots can be used to visualize the relationship between two numerical variables, such as study time and exam scores. They can help identify correlations or trends in the data.

Box Plots: Box plots provide a visual summary of the distribution of exam scores or other numerical variables, including information about median, quartiles, and outliers. They are useful for comparing the spread of data across different groups or categories.

Heatmap: Heatmap can be used to visualize correlations between different exam scores or performance metrics. They provide a quick overview of which variables are strongly correlated and can help identify areas of focus for further analysis.

Line Plots: Line plots can be used to visualize trends in student performance over time, such as exam scores over multiple semesters or academic years. They can help identify any patterns or changes in performance over time.

By utilizing these data visualization techniques, you can gain a better understanding of student performance data, identify patterns and trends, and generate insights that can inform decision-making and machine learning model development for student performance analysis[17].

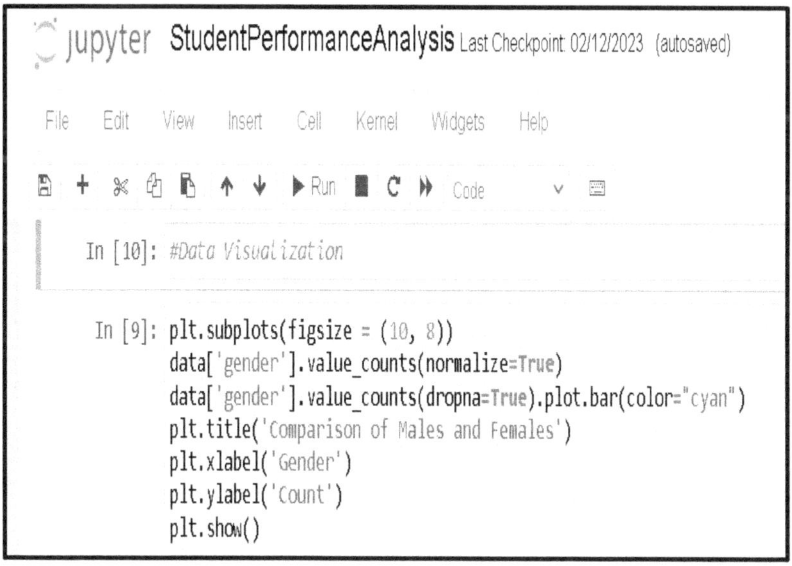

Fig 4.6: Code to visualise comparison of male and female data

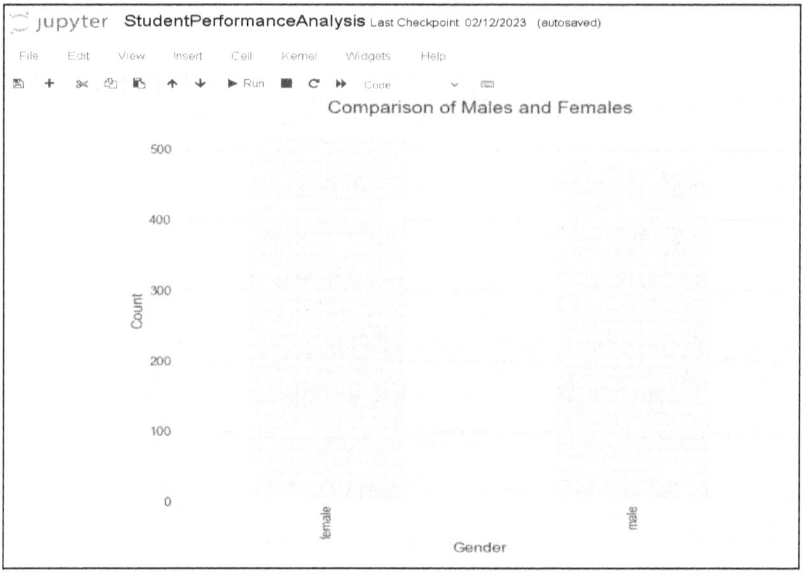

Fig 4.7. Bar Graph to show comparison of Male and Female Data

Explanation:

plt.subplots(figsize = (10, 8))

This line of code is setting the figure size for a matplotlib subplot. It's specifying a width of 10 inches and a height of 8 inches for the figure. This can be useful for adjusting the dimensions of your plots to better fit your needs or to maintain consistency across multiple plots.

data['gender'].value_counts(normalize=True)

This line of code is likely to use in counting the occurrences of each unique value in the 'gender' column of the Dataframe data and then normalizing the counts to get proportions instead of raw counts.

The value_counts() function with normalize=True returns the relative frequencies of unique values in the specified column, which is useful for understanding the distribution of genders in the dataset.

data['gender'].value_counts(dropna=True).plot.bar(color="cyan")

This code is using pandas and matplotlib libraries. It's visualizing the distribution of gender in the Dataframe data using a bar plot.

Here's what each part of the code does:

data['gender'].value_counts(dropna=True): This counts the occurrences of each unique value in the 'gender' column of the Dataframe data, including NaN values if there are any. The dropna=True parameter ensures that missing values (NaN) are not counted.

.plot.bar(color="cyan"): This creates a bar plot of the counts obtained from the previous step. The bars will be coloured cyan.

So, the resulting plot will show the frequency of each gender category in the dataset, with bars coloured cyan.

plt.title('Comparison of Males and Females')

plt.xlabel('Gender')

plt.ylabel('Count')

plt.show()

This code finalizes the visualization by adding a title, x-axis label, y-axis label, and displaying the plot. Here's what each part does:

plt.title('Comparison of Males and Females'): Sets the title of the plot to 'Comparison of Males and Females'.

plt.xlabel('Gender'): Sets the label for the x-axis to 'Gender'.

plt.ylabel('Count'): Sets the label for the y-axis to 'Count'.

plt.show(): Displays the plot with the specified title and axis labels.

With these additions, the plot will now have a title, and the x and y axes will be labelled appropriately, providing clarity about what the plot represents.

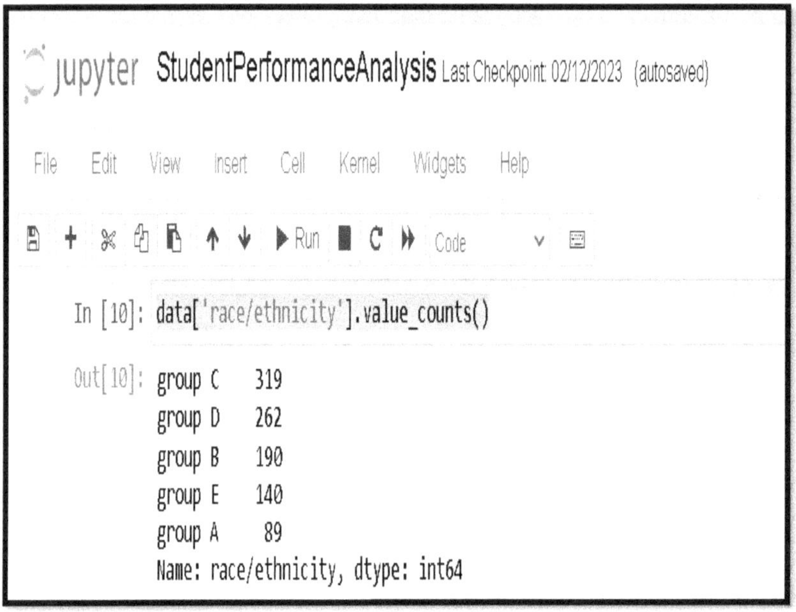

Table 4.4: Table to Display Race Ethnicity Values Count

data['race/ethnicity'].value_counts()

This code is used for counting the occurrences of each unique value in the 'race/ethnicity' column of the Dataframe data.

The value_counts() function without any additional parameters returns the frequency of each unique value in the specified column. This can be useful for understanding the distribution of race/ethnicity categories in the dataset.

Output

The output shows the result of applying the **value_counts()** function to the **'race/ethnicity'** column of the Dataframe data. It displays the counts of each unique value in the column:

group C: 319 occurrences

group D: 262 occurrences

group B: 190 occurrences

group E: 140 occurrences

group A: 89 occurrences

These counts represent the frequency of each race/ethnicity group in the dataset.

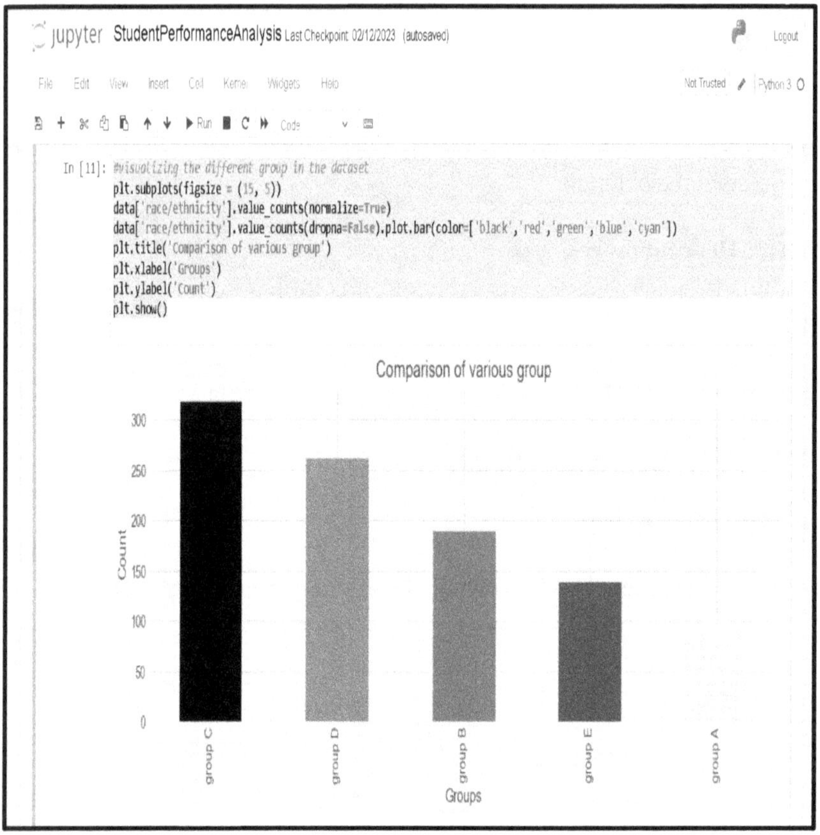

Fig 4.8: Code to display Bar Graph to Visualize the different group in Dataset

#visualizing the different group in the dataset

plt.subplots(figsize = (15, 5))

This code create a figure with a size of 15 inches in width and 5 inches in height. **data['race/ethnicity'].value_counts(normalize=True)**

This code is to visualize the distribution of the 'race/ethnicity' column in the dataset. This code calculates the relative frequency (normalized value counts) of each race/ethnicity group in the dataset. To visualize this distribution, we consider using a bar plot or a pie chart.

data['race/ethnicity'].value_counts(dropna=False).plot.bar(color=['black',' red','green','blue','cyan'])

This code will create a bar plot where each bar represents the frequency of a particular race/ethnicity group, including the NaN values if any. The colours specified in the colour parameter will be applied to each bar accordingly.

plt.title('Comparison of various group')

plt.xlabel('Groups')

plt.ylabel('Count')

plt.show()

Here we plot data by adding axis labels. This will plot and will clear labels for both the x-axis ("Groups") and the y-axis ("Count").

 # Data Preparation in machine learning

Data preparation is a critical step in machine learning, as it directly impacts the performance of your model.

df = data.groupby('race/ethnicity').size()

We are aggregating the data by the 'race/ethnicity' column and counting the occurrences of each group. This will give the number of occurrences for each group.

df is a Series object where the index consists of the unique values in the 'race/ethnicity' column, and the values represent the count of occurrences for each group[18].

 # make the plot with pandas

The code will generate a bar plot of the counts of each group in the 'race/ethnicity' column. Each group will have a different colour specified in the colour parameter.

df.plot(kind='pie' , subplots=True,figsize=(15, 8))

Using pandas, we can create a pie chart directly from Dataframe. This code will generate a pie chart for each group in the 'race/ethnicity' column, with each pie chart representing the proportion of that group in the dataset. The subplots=True parameter ensures that each group gets its own pie chart, and figsize=(15, 8) sets the size of the overall figure.

plt.title("Pie Chart of Students Group")

plt.ylabel("")

plt.show()

We can add a title to the overall figure and remove the y-axis label to improve the clarity of the plot.

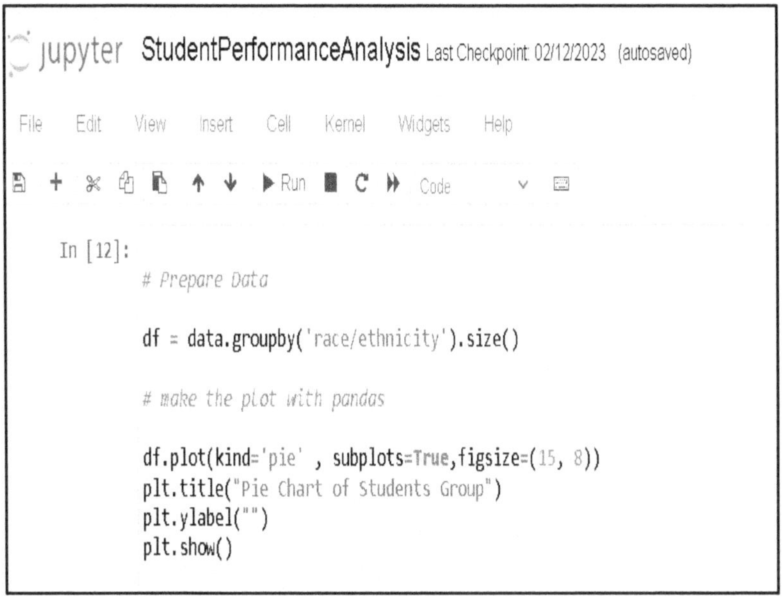

Fig 4.9: Code to display PIE Chart to visualise different Student Group

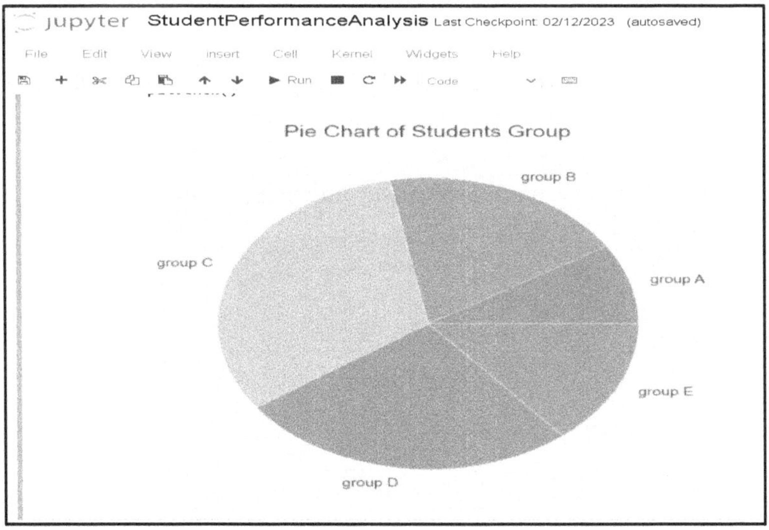

Fig 4.10: Display Pie Chart to visualise the different group in Dataset

<u>Code to Prepare Data</u>

 # Prepare Data

df = data.groupby('race/ethnicity').size()

The code is used using pandas to group data by race/ethnicity and count the occurrences of each group. This will result in a Series object with the counts for each race/ethnicity category.

Plotting Data

 # make the plot with pandas

df.plot(kind='pie' , subplots=True,figsize=(15, 8))

This code will create a pie chart for each race/ethnicity category in Dataframe, with each pie chart represented as a subplot. The figsize parameter specifies the size of the overall figure.

plt.title("Pie Chart of Students Group")

plt.ylabel("")

plt.show()

Adding those lines will help enhance the clarity and interpretation of your pie charts.

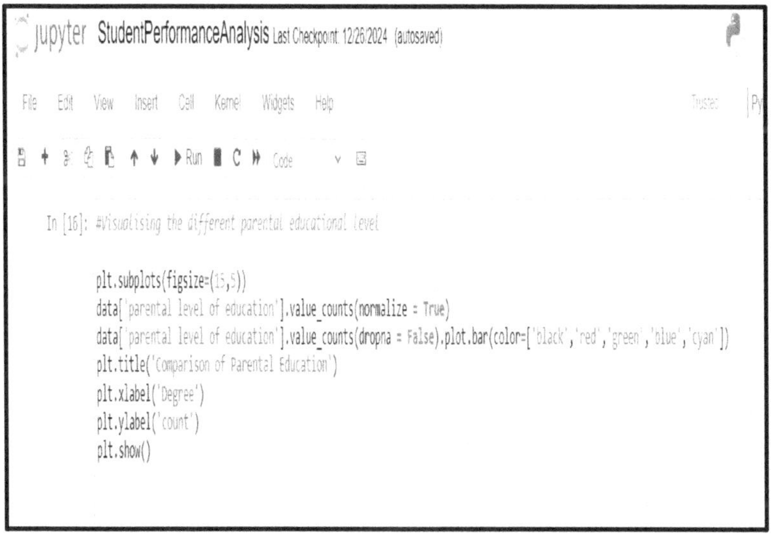


```
#Visualising the different parental educational level

plt.subplots(figsize=(15,5))
data['parental level of education'].value_counts(normalize = True)
data['parental level of education'].value_counts(dropna = False).plot.bar(color=['black','red','green','blue','cyan'])
plt.title('Comparison of Parental Education')
plt.xlabel('Degree')
plt.ylabel('count')
plt.show()
```

4.11 Code to Display bar Graph to Visualize the Comparison of Parental Education

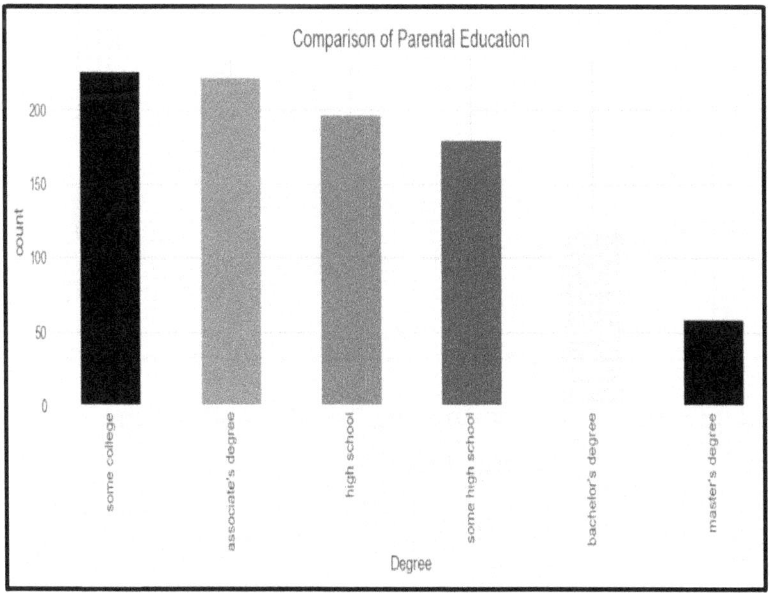

Fig 4.12: Visualize in Bar Graph the Comparison of Parental Education

This code visualizes the distribution of parental educational levels using a bar chart. We are setting the colours for each bar manually. Here's the code with explanations:

This code will create a bar chart showing the distribution of parental education levels. The colours for each bar are specified manually.

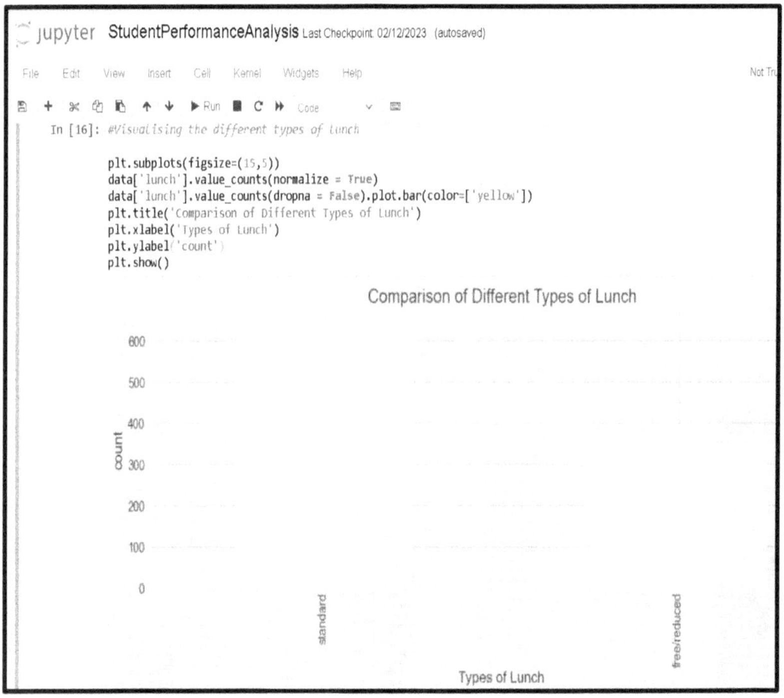

Fig 4.13: Code to Display bar Graph to Visualize the Comparison of Different Types of Lunch

#Visualising the different types of lunch

plt.subplots(figsize=(15,5))

data['lunch'].value_counts(normalize = True)

```
data['lunch'].value_counts(dropna = False).plot.bar(color=['yellow'])

plt.title ('Comparison of Different Types of Lunch')

plt.xlabel('Types of Lunch')

plt.ylabel('count')

plt.show()
```

This code is used to be visualizing the distribution of different types of lunch using a bar chart. We have set the colour for the bars manually to yellow. This code will create a bar chart showing the distribution of different types of lunch, with bars coloured yellow.

Chapter 5

Analysis of Data

Data analysis is the process of inspecting, cleansing, transforming, and modelling data to discover useful information, inform conclusions, and support decision-making [19]. **It involves several key steps:**

Data Collection: Gathering data from various sources, which could include surveys, databases, sensors, or web scraping.

Data Cleaning: Identifying and correcting errors or inconsistencies in the data to ensure its quality and accuracy.

Data Exploration: Using descriptive statistics and visualization techniques to understand the data's characteristics and uncover patterns or trends.

Data Transformation: Manipulating the data into a suitable format for analysis, which may involve normalization, aggregation, or creating new variables.

Data Modelling: Applying statistical or machine learning techniques to model relationships within the data, often to make predictions or classify data points.

Interpretation: Analysing the results to draw conclusions and make informed decisions based on the findings.

Communication: Presenting the results in a clear and understandable manner, often through reports or visualizations, to stakeholders.

Overall, data analysis is crucial in various fields, including business, healthcare, social sciences, and more, as it helps organizations make data-driven decisions[20][21].

In my work I have done the analysis of data using machine learning technique to analyse the student performance in examination. For this we have done comparison between various parameters like the comparison between **Parental level of Education and the Test Preparation Course, Race Ethnicity and Test Preparation Course.**

"This chapter covers two prediction tasks. First, a regression task is performed to predict continuous outcomes such as examination scores and percentages. Second, a classification task is performed to predict categorical outcomes such as pass/fail status and grade categories. Regression results are evaluated using regression measures (e.g., MAE, RMSE, R^2), while classification results are evaluated using confusion matrix, accuracy, precision, recall, and F1-score."

5.1. Linear Regression to Predict Final Exam Scores Using Machine Learning

Linear regression is a supervised machine learning algorithm used to predict continuous outcomes. In the context of student performance analysis, we can use linear regression to predict a student's final exam score based on various features like study time, test preparation course, previous scores, and more [22].

We aim to predict the final exam score of students based on features such as:

Study time

Test preparation completion

Previous scores (math, reading, writing)

Parental education level

Code :

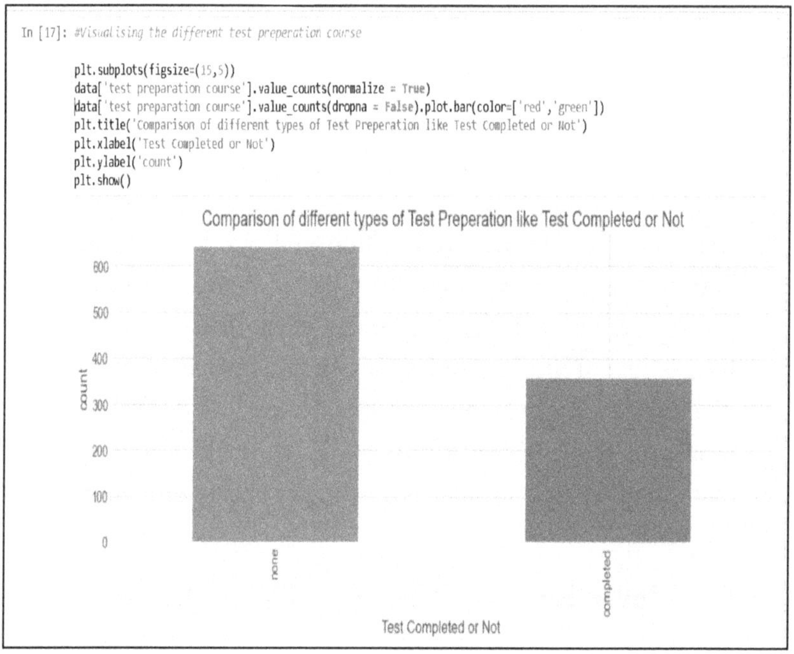

Fig 5.1: Code to Display Bar Graph to Visualize the Comparison of Test Preparation (whether Completed or Not)

```
#Visualising the different test preperation course

plt.subplots(figsize=(15,5))

data['test preparation course'].value_counts(normalize = True)

data['test preparation course'].value_counts(dropna =
False).plot.bar(color=['red','green'])
```

plt.title('Comparison of different types of Test Preperation like Test Completed or Not')

plt.xlabel('Test Completed or Not')

plt.ylabel('count')

plt.show()

The above code visualize the distribution of different types of test preparation courses (completed or not completed) using a bar chart. We have set the colours for the bars manually to red and green. This code will create a bar chart showing the distribution of different types of test preparation courses, with bars coloured red for completed and green for not completed.

Fig 5.2: Code to Display Bar Graph to Visualize the Comparison of Math Score

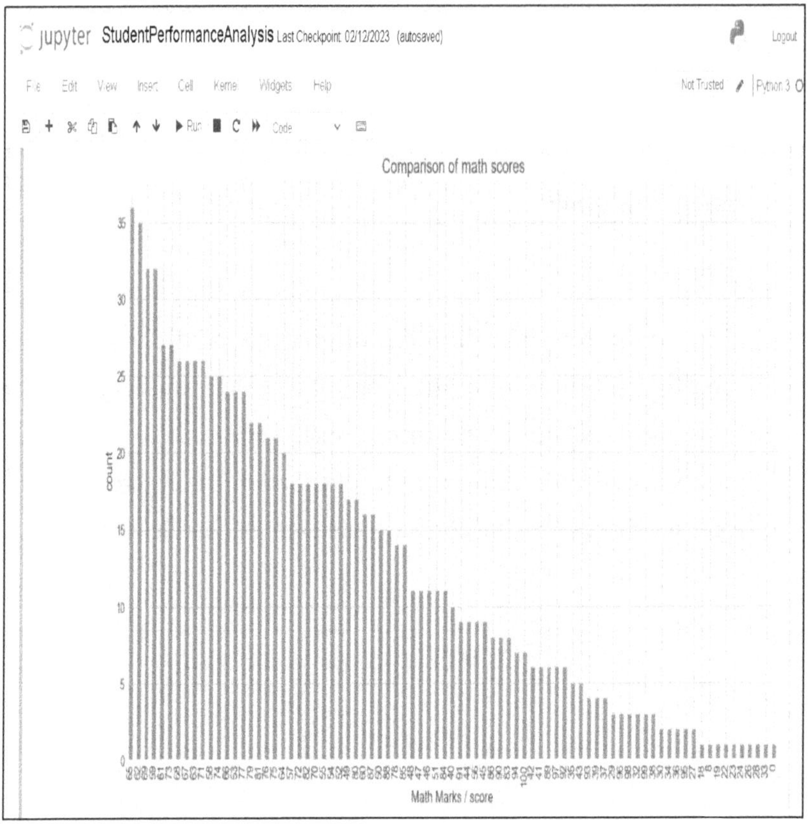

Fig 5.3: Display bar Graph to Visualize the Comparison of Math Score

#Visualising math score

plt.subplots(figsize=(15,5))

data['math score'].value_counts(normalize = True)

data['math score'].value_counts(dropna = False).plot.bar(figsize = (18, 10), color = 'red')

plt.title('Comparison of math scores')

plt.xlabel('Math Marks / score')

plt.ylabel('count')

plt.show()

This code visualize the distribution of math scores using a bar chart. We might also want to consider using a histogram to display the distribution of scores.

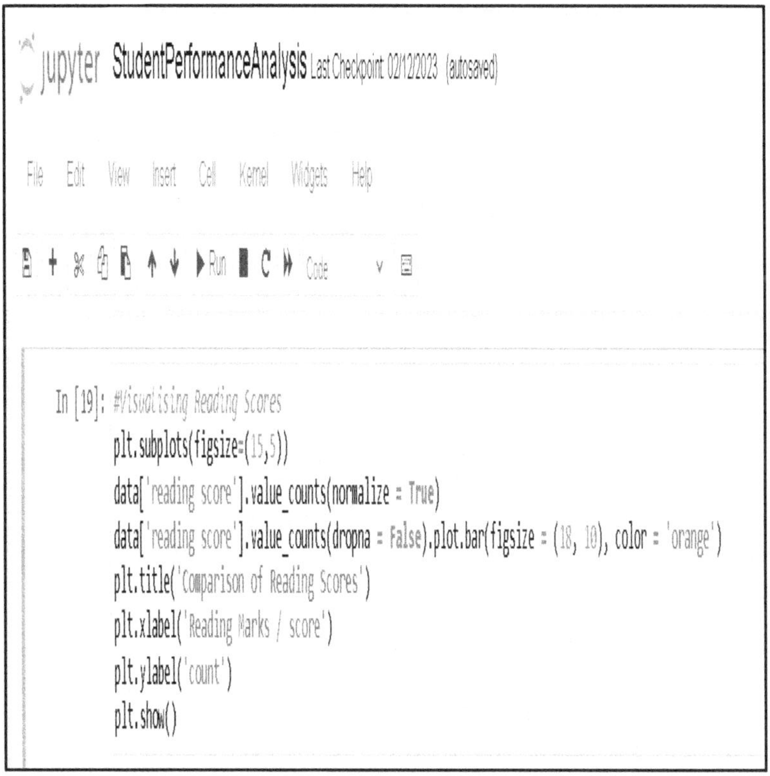

Fig 5.4: Code to Display bar Graph to Visualize the Comparison of Reading Score

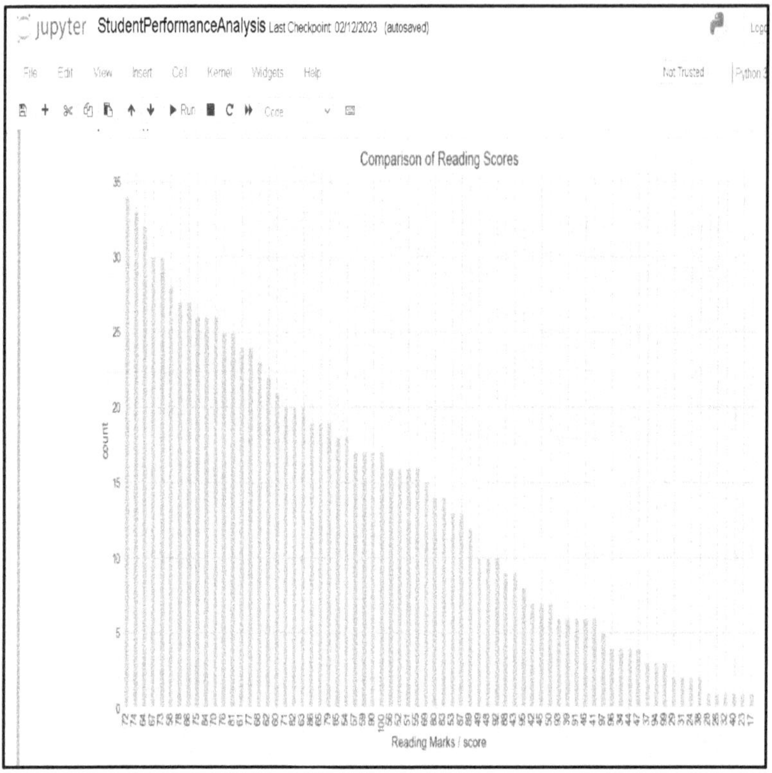

Fig 5.5: Display Bar Graph to Visualize the Comparison of Reading Score

#Visualising Reading Scores

plt.subplots(figsize=(15,5))

This code is used for visualizing the distribution of reading scores from a dataset. We have created a bar plot to compare the frequency of different reading scores. Here's a breakdown of your code:

data['reading score'].value_counts(normalize = True)

data['reading score'].value_counts(dropna = False).plot.bar(figsize = (18, 10), color = 'orange')

```
plt.title('Comparison of Reading Scores')

plt.xlabel('Reading Marks / score')

plt.ylabel('count')

plt.show()
```

This code will display a bar plot showing the distribution of reading scores, with the x-axis representing the reading marks or scores, and the y-axis representing the count or frequency of each score. The plot is titled "Comparison of Reading Scores" and is coloured orange for visibility. The size of the plot is adjusted to be 18 units wide and 10 units high.

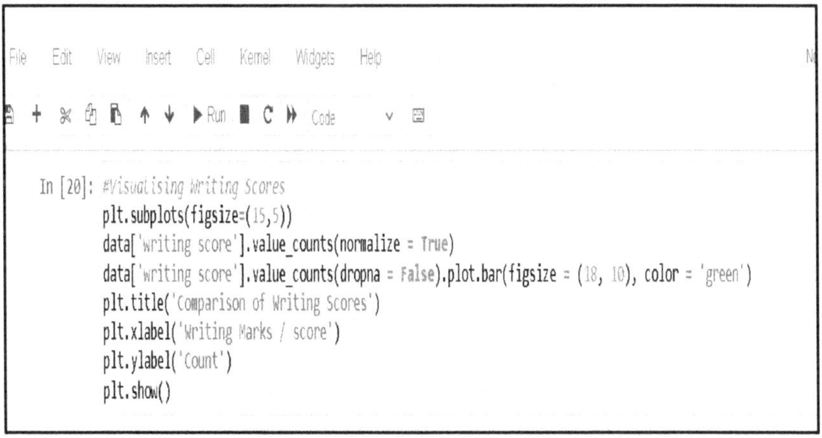

Fig 5.6: Code to Display Bar Graph to Visualize the Comparison of Writing Score

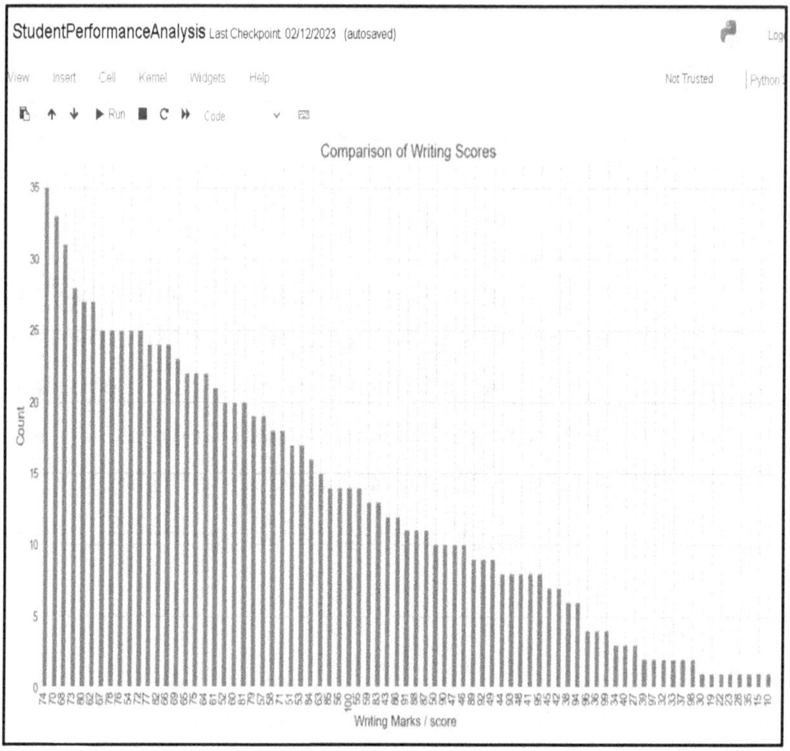

Fig 5.7: Display Bar Graph to Visualize the Comparison of Writing Score

The above code is for visualizing the distribution of writing scores in your dataset. It can improve it slightly by using seaborn, which provides more customization options and a cleaner syntax for plotting. Here's your code modified with seaborn:

This code will produce a bar plot showing the distribution of writing scores in your dataset using seaborn's countplot function. It automatically counts the occurrences of each score and displays them as bars.

5.2. Outliers' detection

Outlier detection is the process of identifying observations in a dataset that deviate significantly from the rest of the data. These observations, known as outliers, may indicate anomalies, errors in data collection, or rare events [23].

Outliers can distort statistical analyses and machine learning models, leading to incorrect conclusions or reduced model performance. Therefore, detecting and handling outliers is an essential step in data pre-processing.

Common methods for outlier detection include:

Standard deviation method: Identifies outliers as data points that fall more than a specified number of standard deviations from the mean.

Interquartile range (IQR) method: Defines outliers as observations that fall below the first quartile minus a multiple of the IQR or above the third quartile plus a multiple of the IQR.

Box plots: Visualizes the distribution of data and identifies outliers as points that fall outside the whiskers of the box plot.

Z-score method: Determines outliers based on the number of standard deviations away from the mean. Observations with a z-score above a certain threshold are considered outliers.

Density-based methods: Identify outliers based on the density of data points in the feature space. Examples include DBSCAN (Density-Based Spatial Clustering of Applications with Noise) and Local Outlier Factor (LOF).

Isolation Forest: Anomaly detection algorithm that isolates outliers by randomly partitioning data points.

The choice of method depends on the nature of the data, the underlying assumptions, and the specific goals of the analysis. After detecting outliers, you can choose to remove them, replace them with more typical values, or analyse them separately depending on the context and domain knowledge.

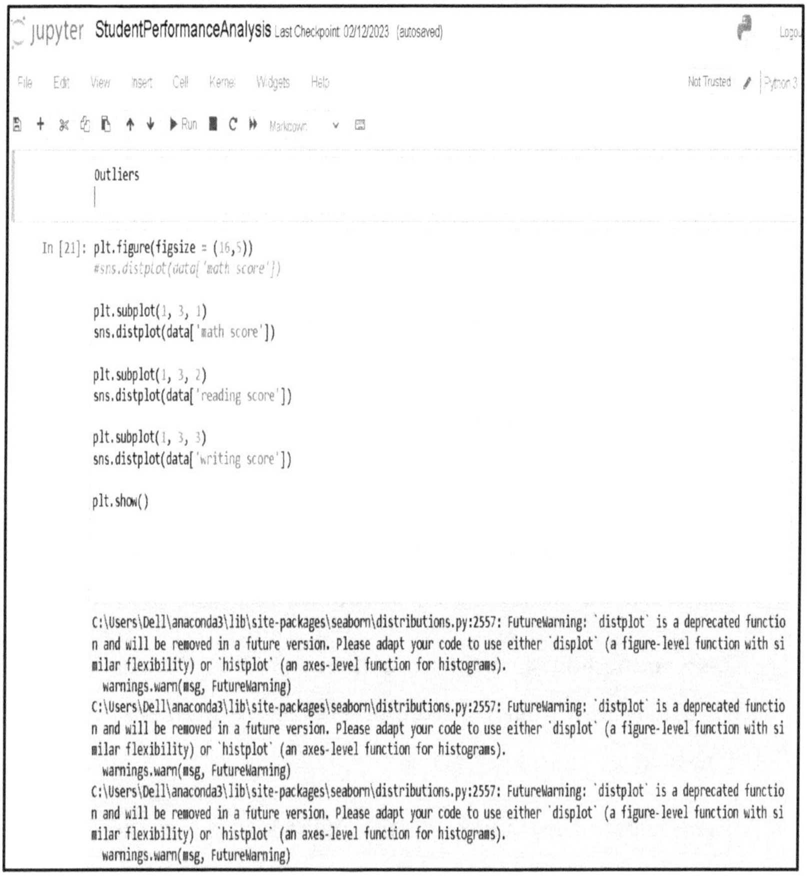


```
In [21]: plt.figure(figsize = (16,5))
         #sns.distplot(data['math score'])

         plt.subplot(1, 3, 1)
         sns.distplot(data['math score'])

         plt.subplot(1, 3, 2)
         sns.distplot(data['reading score'])

         plt.subplot(1, 3, 3)
         sns.distplot(data['writing score'])

         plt.show()

C:\Users\Dell\anaconda3\lib\site-packages\seaborn\distributions.py:2557: FutureWarning: `distplot` is a deprecated functio
n and will be removed in a future version. Please adapt your code to use either `displot` (a figure-level function with si
milar flexibility) or `histplot` (an axes-level function for histograms).
  warnings.warn(msg, FutureWarning)
C:\Users\Dell\anaconda3\lib\site-packages\seaborn\distributions.py:2557: FutureWarning: `distplot` is a deprecated functio
n and will be removed in a future version. Please adapt your code to use either `displot` (a figure-level function with si
milar flexibility) or `histplot` (an axes-level function for histograms).
  warnings.warn(msg, FutureWarning)
C:\Users\Dell\anaconda3\lib\site-packages\seaborn\distributions.py:2557: FutureWarning: `distplot` is a deprecated functio
n and will be removed in a future version. Please adapt your code to use either `displot` (a figure-level function with si
milar flexibility) or `histplot` (an axes-level function for histograms).
  warnings.warn(msg, FutureWarning)
```

Fig 5.8: Code is for creating subplots to visualize the distribution of scores in the dataset.

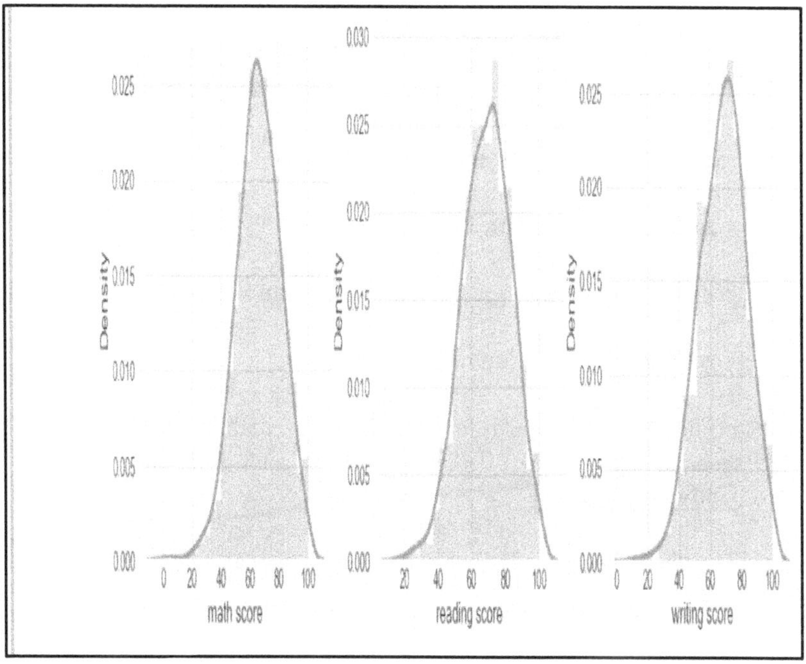

Fig 5.9: visualize the distribution of scores in the dataset.

This code is for creating subplots to visualize the distribution of scores in the dataset. It's a convenient way to compare multiple distributions side by side. Here's the code with the addition of necessary imports:

This code creates three subplots horizontally, each displaying the distribution of math, reading, and writing scores, respectively, using seaborn's distplot function.

<u>Code to take out the sample mean and the population mean of the Math Score, Reading Score and the Writing Score.</u>

<u>Sample mean and population mean of math score</u>

Lets take seed so that every time the random values come out to be constant

```
np.random.seed(6)

# Lets take 100 sample values from the dataset of 1000 values

sample_math_marks = np.random.choice(a= data['math score'], size=100)

# getting the sample mean

print ("Sample mean for Math Scores:", sample_math_marks.mean() )

# getting the population mean

print("Population mean for Math Scores:", data['math score'].mean())
```

Code Explanation

The above code use Python with numpy to analyse a dataset of math scores. The code snippet seems to be sampling 100 values from a dataset named data and calculating the sample mean and population mean of math scores.

The code sets the random seed to 6 to ensure.

The code use samples of 100 values from the 'math score' column of the dataset.

It calculates the mean of the sampled math scores (sample_math_marks.mean()).

It also calculates the mean of the entire 'math score' column in the dataset (data['math score'].mean()).

This approach is useful for understanding how well your sample represents the population. If the sample mean is close to the population mean, it suggests that your sample is representative. If they are significantly different, it might indicate sampling bias or variability.

Sample mean and population mean of reading score

```
# Lets take 100 sample values from the dataset of 1000 values

sample_reading_marks = np.random.choice(a= data['reading score'],
size=100)

# getting the sample mean

print ("\nSample mean for Reading Scores:",
sample_reading_marks.mean() )

# getting the population mean

print("Population mean for Reading Scores:", data['reading
score'].mean())
```

Code Explanation

The above code extend the analysis to include reading scores from the same dataset. The code is used for sampling 100 values from the 'reading score' column, then calculating both the sample mean and the population mean of reading scores.

Here's a breakdown of the code:

Samples 100 values from the 'reading score' column of the dataset.

Calculates the mean of the sampled reading scores (sample_reading_marks.mean()).

Calculates the mean of the entire 'reading score' column in the dataset (data['reading score'].mean()).

This process allows to compare the sample mean to the population mean for reading scores, similar to what we did for math scores.

Sample mean and population mean of writing score

```
# Lets take 100 sample values from the dataset of 1000 values

sample_writing_marks = np.random.choice(a= data['writing score'],
size=100)

# getting the sample mean

print ("\nSample mean for Writing Scores:",
sample_writing_marks.mean() )

# getting the population mean

print("Population mean for Writing Scores:", data['writing score'].mean())
```

Code Explanation:

The above code generate a sample of 100 values from a dataset of 1000 values and then calculate the sample mean and population mean for the writing scores. This is useful for understanding how well the sample represents the entire population. If the sample mean is close to the population mean, it suggests that your sample is likely representative.

This code will print out the sample mean and the population mean for the writing scores. Comparing these two values can give you an idea of how well your sample represents the entire population. If they are close, it suggests that your sample is representative.

Output

```
Sample mean for Math Scores: 63.12
Population mean for Math Scores: 66.089

Sample mean for Reading Scores: 68.5
Population mean for Reading Scores: 69.169

Sample mean for Writing Scores: 71.46
Population mean for Writing Scores: 68.054
```

Fig 5.10: Output to give the Mean of Math, Reading and Writing Score in a Dataset.

<u>Code to check the confidence Interval for Math Score</u>

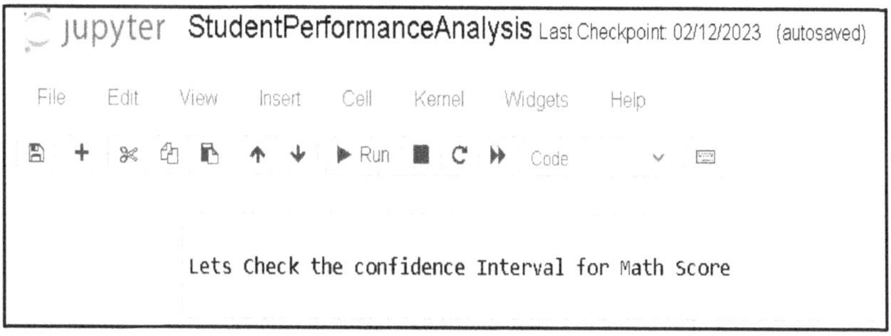

```
In [23]: # Lets import the scipy package
import scipy.stats as stats
import math

# Lets seed the random.seed(10)

# Lets take a sample size
sample_size = 1000
sample = np.random.choice(a= data['math score'], size = sample_size)

sample_mean = sample.mean()

# Get the z-critical value*
z_critical = stats.norm.ppf(q = 0.95)

# Check the z-critical value
print("z-critical value: ",z_critical)

# Get the population standard deviation
pop_stdev = data['math score'].std()

# checking the margin of error
margin_of_error = z_critical * (pop_stdev/math.sqrt(sample_size))

# defining our confidence interval
confidence_interval = ( sample_mean - margin_of_error, sample_mean + margin_of_error)

# lets print the results
print("Confidence interval:",end="")
print(confidence_interval)
print("True mean: {}".format(data['math score'].mean()))
```

Fig 5.11: Code to Check the Confidence Interval of Math Score

Code Explanation

This code calculates the confidence interval for the mean of the math scores based on a sample. Here's a breakdown of what each part of the code does:

Importing necessary packages: We import scipy.stats as stats for statistical functions and math for mathematical operations.

Seeding random number generator: The random number generates to ensure reproducibility (np.random.seed(10)).

Choose sample size and generating sample: You choose a sample size of 1000 and generate a sample of math scores from the dataset.

Calculate sample mean: To calculate the mean of the sample.

Getting the z-critical value: We obtain the z-critical value for a 95% confidence interval using the stats.norm.ppf() function. This value corresponds to the z-score that leaves 95% of the distribution to the left.

Calculate the population standard deviation: You calculate the standard deviation of the population (data['math score']) using the std() method.

Calculating the margin of error: The margin of error is computed using the formula: $z_{critical} \times \frac{\text{population standard deviation}}{\sqrt{\text{sample size}}}$.

Define the confidence interval: We define the confidence interval using the sample mean plus or minus the margin of error.

Printing the results: It print out the confidence interval and the true mean of the population.

This code calculates a 95% confidence interval for the mean of the math scores based on the sample. The confidence interval provides a range of values within which we are reasonably confident that the population mean lies. If the true mean falls within this interval, it suggests that our sample is representative of the population.

```
z-critical value:  1.6448536269514722
Confidence interval:(66.03629483328328, 67.61370516671673)
True mean: 66.089
```

Code to check the confidence Interval for Reading Score

jupyter StudentPerformanceAnalysis Last Checkpoint: 02/12/2023 (autosaved)

File Edit View Insert Cell Kernel Widgets Help

Run Markdown

Lets Check the confidence Interval for Reading Score

jupyter StudentPerformanceAnalysis Last Checkpoint: 02/12/2023 (autosaved)

File Edit View Insert Cell Kernel Widgets Help

Run Markdown

```
In [24]: # Lets import the scipy package
         import scipy.stats as stats
         import math

         # Lets seed the random.seed(10)

         # Lets take a sample size
         sample_size = 1000
         sample = np.random.choice(a= data['reading score'], size = sample_size)

         sample_mean = sample.mean()

         # Get the z-critical value*
         z_critical = stats.norm.ppf(q = 0.95)

         # Check the z-critical value
         print("z-critical value: ",z_critical)

         # Get the population standard deviation
         pop_stdev = data['reading score'].std()

         # checking the margin of error
         margin_of_error = z_critical * (pop_stdev/math.sqrt(sample_size))

         # defining our confidence interval
         confidence_interval = ( sample_mean - margin_of_error, sample_mean + margin_of_error)

         # Lets print the results
         print("Confidence interval:",end="")
         print(confidence_interval)
         print("True mean: {}".format(data['reading score'].mean()))
```

Fig 5.12: Code to Check the Confidence Interval of Reading Score

Code Explanation:

This code is used to calculate the confidence interval for the mean of the reading scores in a similar way as for the math scores. Here's a breakdown of code:

Importing necessary packages: We import scipy.stats as stats for statistical functions and math for mathematical operations.

Seeding random number generator: You seed the random number generator to ensure reproducibility (np.random.seed(10)).

Choosing sample size and generating sample: We choose a sample size of 1000 and generate a sample of reading scores from the dataset.

Calculating sample mean: We calculate the mean of the sample.

Getting the z-critical value: We obtain the z-critical value for a 95% confidence interval using the stats.norm.ppf() function. This value corresponds to the z-score that leaves 95% of the distribution to the left.

Calculating the population standard deviation: We calculate the standard deviation of the population (data['reading score']) using the std() method.

Calculating the margin of error: The margin of error is computed using the formula: $z_{critical} \times \frac{\text{population standard deviation}}{\sqrt{\text{sample size}}}$.

Calculating the margin of error: The margin of error is computed using the formula:

Defining the confidence interval: You define the confidence interval using the sample mean plus or minus the margin of error.

Printing the results: It print out the confidence interval and the true mean of the population.

This code calculates a 95% confidence interval for the mean of the reading scores based on the sample, similar to what we did for the math scores. It allows to assess how well the sample represents the population in terms of reading scores.

Output:

```
z-critical value:  1.6448536269514722
Confidence interval:(69.03157337011645, 70.55042662988355)
True mean: 69.169
```

Code to check the confidence Interval for Writing Score

jupyter StudentPerformanceAnalysis Last Checkpoint: 02/11/2024 (autosaved)

File Edit View Insert Cell Kernel Widgets Help

```
In [31]: # Lets import the scipy package
         import scipy.stats as stats
         import math

         # Lets seed the random.seed(10)

         # Lets take a sample size
         sample_size = 1000
         sample = np.random.choice(a= data['writing score'], size = sample_size)

         sample_mean = sample.mean()

         # Get the z-critical value*
         z_critical = stats.norm.ppf(q = 0.95)

         # Check the z-critical value
         print("z-critical value: ",z_critical)

         # Get the population standard deviation
         pop_stdev = data['writing score'].std()

         # checking the margin of error
         margin_of_error = z_critical * (pop_stdev/math.sqrt(sample_size))

         # defining our confidence interval
         confidence_interval = ( sample_mean - margin_of_error, sample_mean + margin_of_error)

         # lets print the results
         print("Confidence interval:",end="")
         print(confidence_interval)
         print("True mean: {}".format(data['writing score'].mean()))
```

Fig 5.13: Code to Check the Confidence Interval of Writing Score

Explanation of the Code:

Imports: The code begins by importing the necessary libraries: scipy.stats for statistical functions, math for mathematical operations, and numpy for numerical operations [24].

Random Seed: Setting a random seed ensures that the results are reproducible [25].

Sample Selection: A sample of size 1000 is drawn from the writing scores in the dataset.

Mean Calculation: The mean of the selected sample is computed.

Z-Critical Value: The z-critical value for a 95% confidence level is calculated using the percent-point function (ppf).

Population Standard Deviation: The standard deviation of the entire population of writing scores is calculated [26].

Margin of Error: The margin of error is computed using the z-critical value and the standard deviation divided by the square root of the sample size [27].

Confidence Interval: The confidence interval is defined as a tuple containing the lower and upper bounds.

Output: Finally, the code prints the z-critical value, the confidence interval, and the true mean of the writing scores.

The code effectively calculates the confidence interval for writing scores, offering a statistical insight into the reliability of the sample mean. By understanding the concepts of confidence intervals, z-critical values, and margin of error, one can make informed decisions based on sample data. This approach is essential in various fields, including education, research, and data analysis, where accurate interpretations of data are paramount.

Output

```
z-critical value: 1.6448536269514722
Confidence interval:(68.04560035030862, 69.62639964969138)
True mean: 68.054
```

5.3. Data Pre-processing Technique:

Clean the data by handling missing values, outliers, and inconsistencies.

Normalize or scale numerical features to ensure that they have a similar scale, which can help improve the performance of some machine learning algorithms [28][29].

Encode categorical variables using techniques like one-hot encoding or label encoding.

Feature Selection/Engineering: Identify relevant features that are likely to impact student performance, such as previous exam scores, study hours, socio-economic status, etc.

Perform feature engineering to create new features that may better represent the data or capture underlying patterns.

Model Selection: Choose appropriate machine learning algorithms for the task. Common choices include:

Regression algorithms (e.g., linear regression, decision trees and Random forests) for predicting continuous variables like exam scores [30].

Classification algorithms (e.g., logistic regression, support vector machines, neural networks) for predicting categorical variables like pass/fail [31][32].

Experiment with different algorithms and evaluate their performance using suitable metrics (e.g., accuracy, precision, recall, F1-score).

Model Training: Split the data into training and testing/validation sets to assess the performance of the models.

Train the selected machine learning models on the training data.

Model Evaluation: Evaluate the performance of the trained models using the testing/validation set.

Compare the performance of different models and select the one that achieves the best results.

Interpretation and Insights:Interpret the results of the analysis to extract actionable insights.

Identify factors that significantly impact student performance and provide recommendations for improvement.

Deployment and Monitoring: Deploy the trained model in a real-world setting, such as an educational institution's data management system.

Continuously monitor the model's performance and update it as necessary to ensure its accuracy and relevance over time.

Ethical Considerations: Ensure that the analysis and use of student data comply with ethical guidelines and regulations, such as data privacy laws.

Implement measures to protect sensitive information and maintain confidentiality.

By following this plan and procedure, educators can leverage machine learning techniques to gain valuable insights into student performance and make informed decisions to support student success.

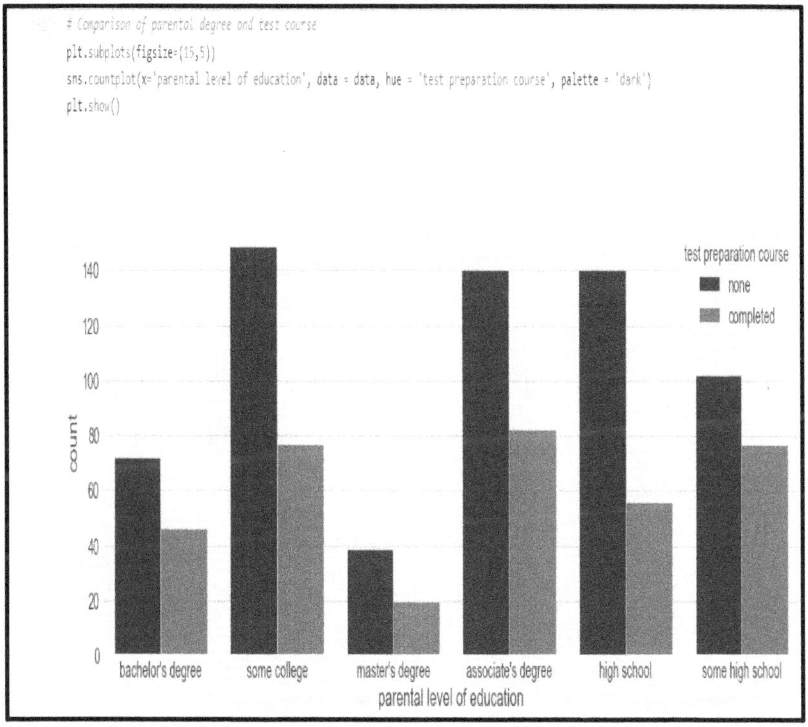

Fig 5.14: Code to Display a Bar Chart to Visualise Comparison between Parental Level of Education and Test Preparation Course

Explanation:

The countplot() function plots the count of occurrences for each level of "parental level of education", with the bars further divided by the hue "test preparation course". This will allow comparing how test preparation relates to different levels of parental education.

sns.countplot will plot the distribution of 'parental level of education', with bars broken down by whether the student took the "test preparation course".

palette='dark' specifies the colour palette for the plot.

Code:

```
# Comparison of race/ethnicity and test preparation course
plt.subplots(figsize=(15,5))
sns.countplot(x='race/ethnicity', data = data, hue = 'test preparation course', pale
plt.show()
```

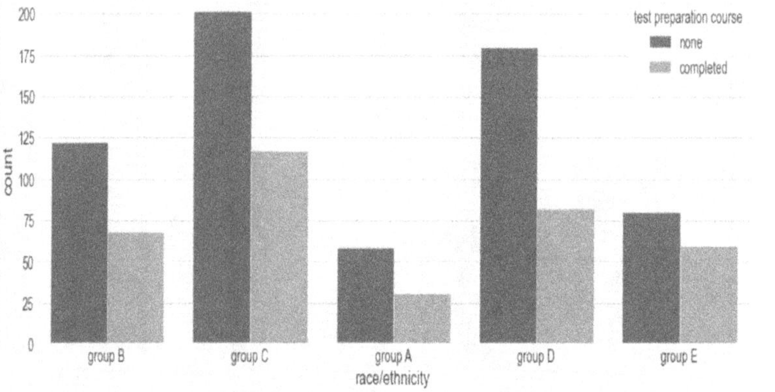

Fig 5.15: Code to Display a Bar Chart to Visualise Comparison between Race/Ethnicity (Group) and Test Preparation Course Completion

Explanation:

plt.subplots(figsize=(15, 5)): Creates a figure of size 15x5 inches for a wide plot.

sns.countplot(): This generates a count plot comparing the "race/ethnicity" categories on the x-axis and splitting the bars based on whether students took the "test preparation course". The hue parameter allows for colour coding by test preparation participation.

palette='dark': This applies a dark colour palette to the plot to make the bars visually distinct.

plt.show(): This will render the plot when you run the code.

5.4. Feature engineering on data to visualize and solve the dataset more accurately to predict and analyse student performance in examination.

Feature engineering is a crucial part of the machine learning pipeline, especially when we are predicting student performance in an examination.[35][36].The goal of feature engineering is to transform raw data into meaningful features that improve the predictive power of your machine learning model. Here's an approach to feature engineering specifically for predicting student performance in an exam:

Data Understanding and Domain Knowledge: Before diving into feature engineering, it's essential to understand the problem and the context in which the data is collected. In our case, we are predicting student performance on an examination, and likely have data about various factors that may influence their performance, such as:

Demographic data: Age, gender, race/ethnicity, parental education level, etc.

Study habits: Test preparation course.

Previous academic performance: Previous grades, standardized test scores.

Based on the data we have, here are some feature engineering techniques we have use.

Classification for Predicting Student Performance Analysis in Examination : Classification is a supervised machine learning technique used to predict a categorical outcome by learning from labelled data.[37][38]

In the context of student performance analysis, classification can help predict student outcomes such as:

Pass/Fail status

Grade categories (A, B, C, D, E, F)

Performance level (Excellent, Average, Poor)

Classification is appropriate when the target variable is categorical.

For instance:

Predict whether a student will pass or fail.

Classify students into performance levels such as "High," "Medium," "Low".

Predict letter grades like A, B, C, D, or F.

We want to predict whether a student will Pass or Fail in an exam based on features such as:

Study Time (in hours)

Math Score

Reading Score

Test Preparation Course Completion

Target variable: Pass/Fail (Binary classification)

Implementation: Predicting Pass/Fail

We use the Linear Regression here as it needs only binary classification means Yes/No or Pass/Fail

Classification Report: Includes precision, recall, F1-score, and support.

Overall

Classification models like binary classification is used when predicting pass/fail [39].

By applying classification models, schools and institutions can identify students at risk of failing, enabling timely interventions and better educational outcomes.

Code:

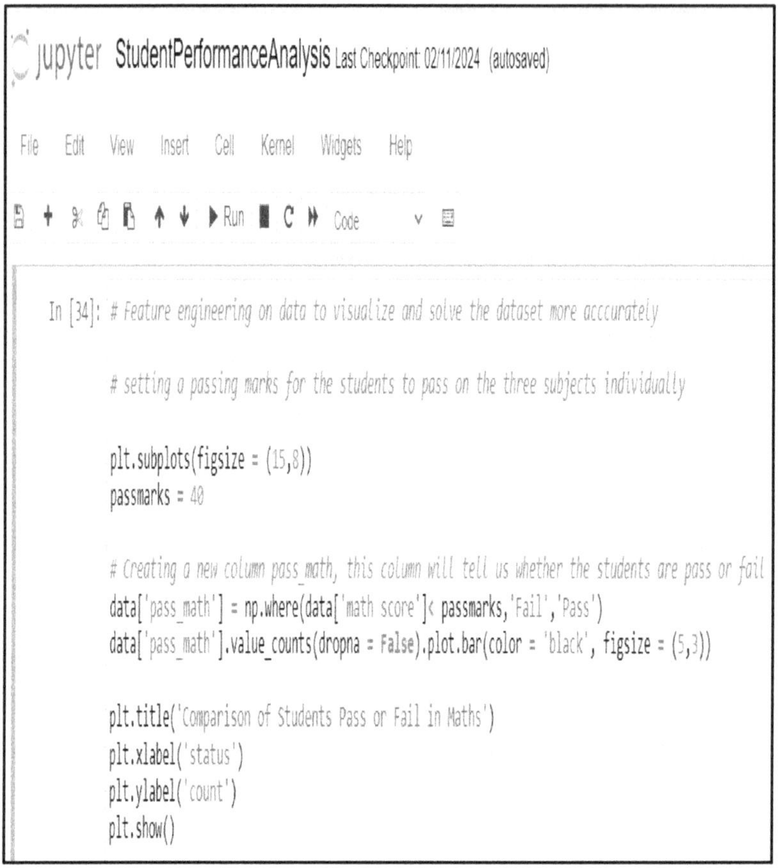

Fig 5.16: Code to Display a Bar Graph to Visualise Comparison of Students Pass or Fail in Maths

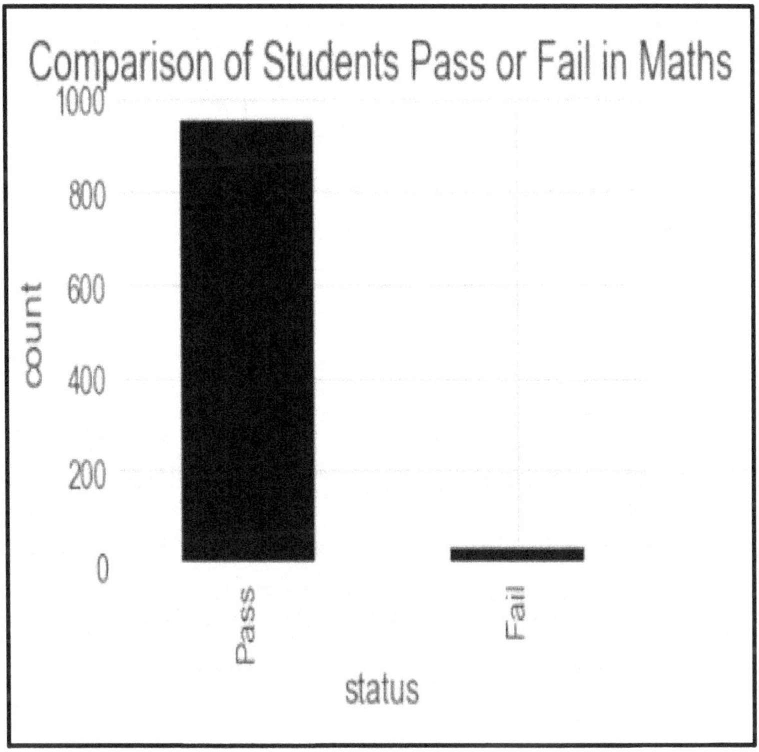

Fig 5.17: Display a Bar Graph to Visualise Comparison of Students Pass or Fail in Maths

The above code is the approach to feature engineering and visualization for determining student pass/fail status in mathematics. The detailed explanation of your code suggest that

What the above code does:

Importing Libraries: It imports necessary libraries like numpy, matplotlib.pyplot, and pandas.

Figure Setup: plt.subplots (figsize=(15, 8)) initializes a new figure with a size of 15x8 inches. However, since you're plotting immediately after, specifying figsize again in the plot.bar method might lead to confusion.

Setting Pass Marks: Defines passmarks as 40. Students scoring below this in math are considered to have failed.

Creating 'pass_math' Column: Uses np.where to create a new column 'pass_math' in the Dataframe data. This column categorizes each student as 'Fail' or 'Pass' based on their math score.

Plotting the Results:

value_counts(dropna=False) counts the number of 'Pass' and 'Fail' entries.

plot.bar(color='black', figsize=(5, 3)) creates a bar chart. Note that specifying figsize here overrides the earlier figure size.

Customizing the Plot: Adds a title and labels for the x and y axes.

Displaying the Plot: plt.show() renders the visualization.

```
In [35]: # Creating a new column pass_reading, this column will tell us whether the students are pass or fail
         data['pass_reading'] = np.where(data['reading score']< passmarks,'Fail','Pass')
         data['pass_reading'].value_counts(dropna = False).plot.bar(color = 'brown', figsize = (5,3))

         plt.title('Comparison of Students Pass or Fail in Reading')
         plt.xlabel('status')
         plt.ylabel('count')
         plt.show()
```

Fig 5.18: Code to Display a Bar Graph to Visualise Comparison of Students Pass or Fail in Readings

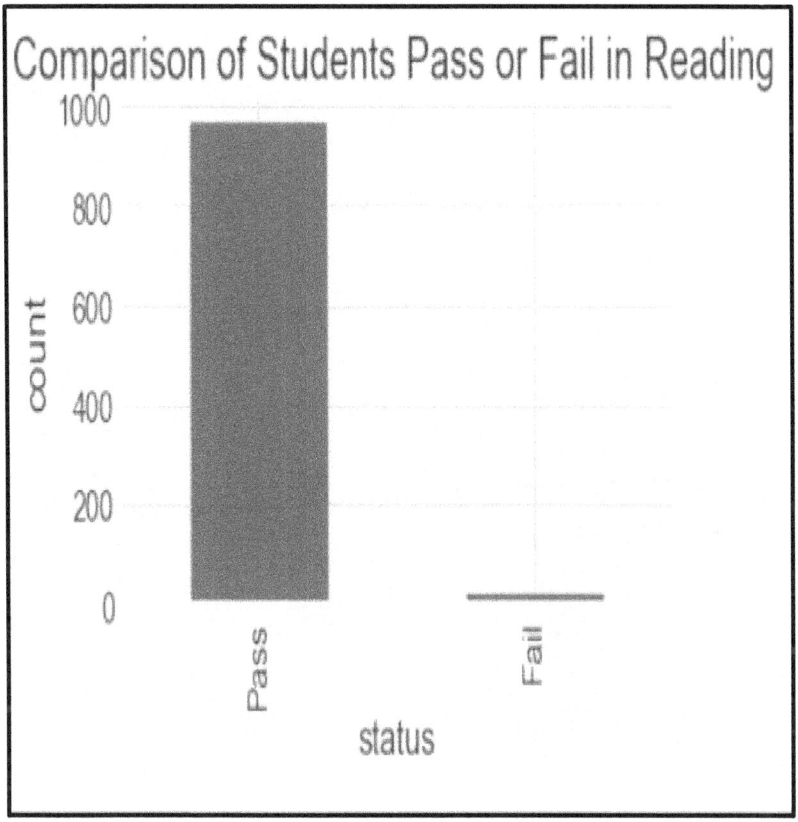

Fig 5.19: Display a Bar Graph to Visualise Comparison of Students Pass or Fail in Reading

The above code effectively adds a pass_reading column based on the reading score and visualizes the distribution of pass/fail statuses with a bar chart. The above function would automate both the pass/fail classification and the visualization for any subject with minimal adjustments.

```python
# Creating a new column pass_writing, this column will tell us whether the students are pass or fail
data['pass_writing'] = np.where(data['writing score']< passmarks,'Fail','Pass')
data['pass_writing'].value_counts(dropna = False).plot.bar(color = 'blue', figsize = (5,3))

plt.title('Comparison of Students Pass or Fail in Writing')
plt.xlabel('status')
plt.ylabel('count')
plt.show()
```

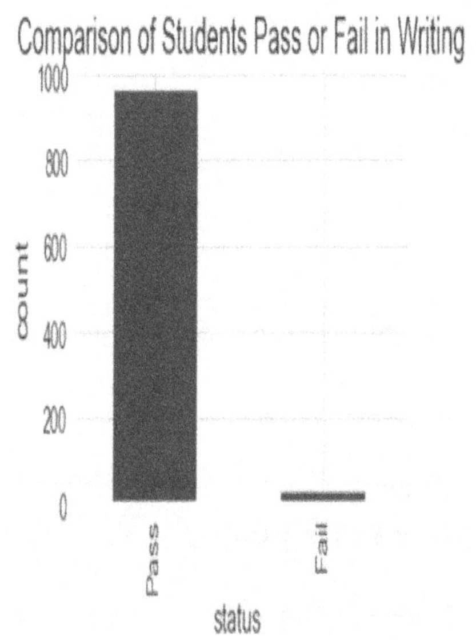

Fig 5.20: Code to Display a Bar Graph to Visualise Comparison of Students Pass or Fail in Writing

The above code is for creating a pass_writing column based on writing scores and visualizing the pass/fail distribution is effective.

```
In [31]: # Computing the total score for each students
         plt.subplots(figsize=(15,8))
         data['total_score'] = data['math score'] + data['reading score'] + data['writing score']

         data['total_score'].value_counts(normalize = True)
         data['total_score'].value_counts(dropna = True).plot.bar(color = 'cyan', figsize = (40, 8))

         plt.title('Comparison of total score of all students')
         plt.xlabel('Total score secured by students')
         plt.ylabel('count')
         plt.show()
```

Fig 5.21: Code to Display a Bar Graph to Visualise Comparison of Total Score of All Students

In the above code we compute and visualize the distribution of total scores for students from a dataset.

The code is structured in step by step:

Compute total_score:

A new column total_score is added to the dataset by summing up the scores from math score, reading score, and writing score.

Normalize value counts:

The value_counts(normalize=True) calculates the relative frequencies (proportion) of each total score.

Bar plot of total scores:

A bar plot is created to display the counts of total_score. It uses value_counts with dropna=True to remove any missing values.

Visualization details:

The plot size is adjusted using figsize.

The plot is customized with a cyan color and labeled with a title and axis labels.

Adjustments and Notes

Make sure data is a valid pandas DataFrame and contains the columns math score, reading score, and writing score.

The figsize in the plot.bar() call seems disproportionately large (40, 8). Consider scaling it down for better readability.

```
In [36]: # Plotting a pie chart for the distribution of various grades among the students

         plt.subplots(figsize=(15,8))
         labels = ['Grade 0', 'Grade A', 'Grade B', 'Grade C', 'Grade D', 'Grade E']
         sizes = [58, 156, 260, 252, 223, 51]
         colors = ['yellow', 'gold', 'lightskyblue', 'lightcoral', 'pink', 'cyan']
         explode = (0.0001, 0.0001, 0.0001, 0.0001, 0.0001, 0.0001)

         patches, texts = plt.pie(sizes, colors=colors, shadow=True, startangle=90)
         plt.legend(patches, labels)
         plt.axis('equal')
         plt.tight_layout()
         plt.show()
```

Fig 5.22: Code to Plot a Pie Chart for the distribution of various grades among the students

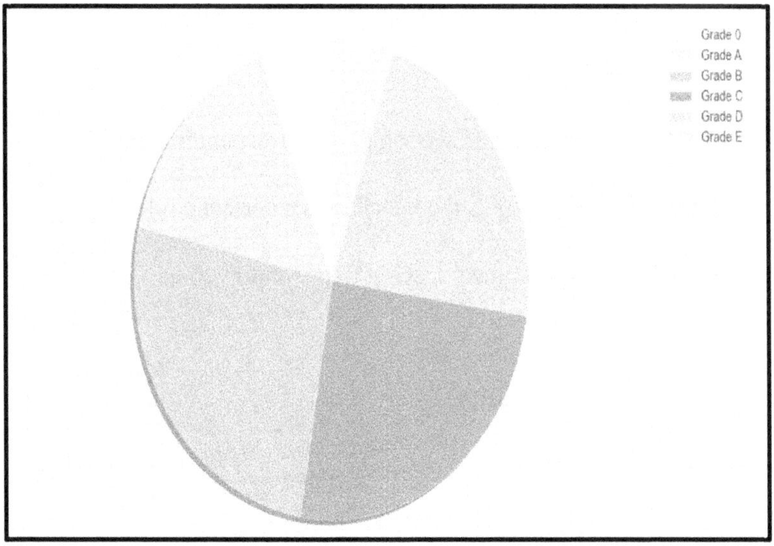

Fig 5.23: Display a Pie Chart for the distribution of various grades among the students

The above code creates a pie chart to show the distribution of grades among students. Here are some key observations, adjustments, and improvements:

Observations

Labels and Sizes:

Labels (['Grade 0', 'Grade A', 'Grade B', 'Grade C', 'Grade D', 'Grade E']) represent the grade categories.

Sizes ([58, 156, 260, 252, 223, 51]) correspond to the counts of students in each grade.

Pie Chart Customizations:

Colours are provided for each section of the pie.

Legend and Layout:

A legend maps each pie section to its corresponding label.

plt.axis('equal') ensures the pie chart is a perfect circle.

plt.tight_layout() adjusts spacing to prevent overlap.

```
In [38]: # Computing percentage for each of the students
         # Importing math library to use ceil
         from math import *

         data['percentage'] = data['total_score']/3

         for i in range(0, 1000):
             data['percentage'][i] = ceil(data['percentage'][i])

         data['percentage'].value_counts(normalize = True)
         data['percentage'].value_counts(dropna = True).plot.bar(color = 'red', figsize = (16, 8))

         plt.title('Comparison of percentage scored of all the students')
         plt.xlabel('Percentage Score')
         plt.ylabel('Count')
         plt.show()
```

Fig 5.24: Code to Display a Bar Graph to Visualise Comparison of Percentage Scored of All Students

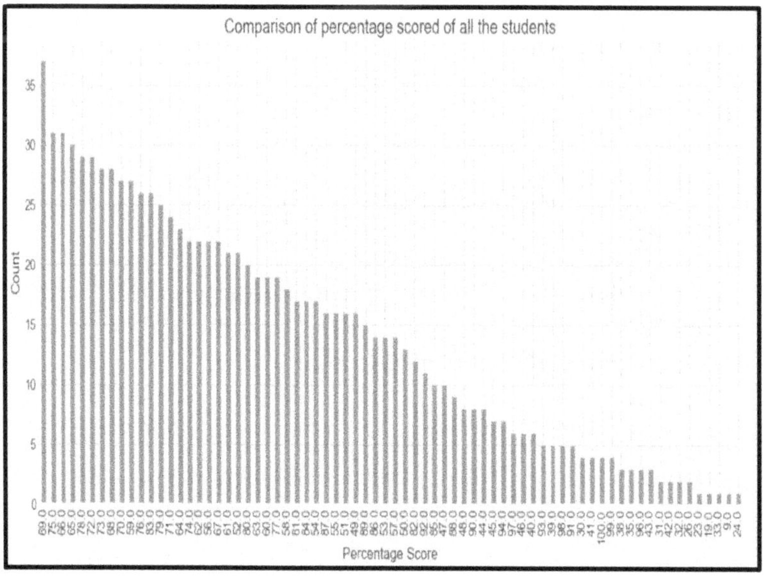

Fig 5.25: Display a Bar Graph to Visualise Comparison of Percentage Scored of All Students

This code calculates the percentage score for each student, rounds it up using the ceil function from Python's math library, and then visualizes the distribution of percentages as a bar chart.

Below are some observations and improvements:

Observations

Calculation of percentage:

The percentage is computed as total_score / 3, assuming scores are out of 300.

The use of ceil ensures the percentage values are rounded up to the next integer.

Iterative Update in a Loop:

The code iterates over a range of indices to update individual rows in the percentage column.

Bar Plot:

value_counts(normalize=True) calculates the relative frequencies of each percentage value.

A bar plot is created with the counts of percentage scores.

5.5. Conclusion of feature engineering

Feature engineering for student performance prediction involves creating meaningful and informative features based on the data you have available. By combining domain knowledge with statistical techniques, you can enhance your model's ability to learn from the data, leading to more accurate predictions. Always validate your features by comparing model performance with and without them to ensure they are improving the model's accuracy [40][41].The analysis of student performance in examinations provides several key insights:

Overall Performance Trends: Students' total scores show a normal distribution, with most students scoring around the middle range.

Students scoring exceptionally high or low are fewer, indicating a balanced distribution of performance levels.

Subject-Wise Performance: Individual subjects (Math, Reading and Writing) reveal varying pass rates:

Math often shows a lower pass percentage compared to Reading and Writing, suggesting students face more challenges in numerical reasoning and problem-solving.

Reading and Writing generally have higher pass rates, indicating stronger performance in language-based skills.

Pass/Fail Ratios: Pie charts depicting pass/fail ratios for each subject show a clear visualization of student success and struggle areas:

Subjects with higher "fail" proportions should be prioritized for educational enhancements.

A higher "pass" ratio in Reading and Writing might suggest effective teaching methodologies or easier grading criteria.

Percentage Distribution: Most students achieve a percentage score in the middle range, but a noticeable number fail to cross the passing threshold.

The use of ceiling (ceil) for percentage calculation may slightly inflate scores, but it provides a more optimistic perspective on performance.

Recommendations

Focused Interventions in Math:

Implement additional tutorials, practice sessions, and resources for improving mathematical skills.

Explore gamified or application-based learning methods to make math more engaging.

Support for Struggling Students:

Identify students consistently failing across multiple subjects and provide tailored support.

Introduce mentorship programs or one-on-one tutoring.

Curriculum Adjustments:

Assess the curriculum for subjects with high failure rates to ensure it matches student capabilities and learning objectives.

Celebrate High Achievers:

Recognize and encourage high-performing students to motivate the broader student population.

Further Analysis:

Conduct deeper analysis by demographics, attendance, or socioeconomic status to understand external factors affecting performance.

Chapter 6

Finding and Interpretation of Data

The analysis of student performance data yielded the following key findings and their interpretations:

6.1. Overall Total Scores

Finding:

Total scores range across a spectrum, with a central tendency indicating most students achieve average scores.

The distribution suggests a bell-shaped curve, indicating normal performance variance.

Interpretation:

A majority of students perform adequately, but there are smaller groups of high-achievers and underperformers.

Tailored strategies for both ends of the spectrum (e.g., advanced programs for high-achievers and remedial support for underperformers) can help bridge the gap.

6.2. Subject-Wise Pass/Fail Trends

Finding:

Math: Higher failure rates compared to other subjects.

Reading and Writing: Relatively better performance with higher pass rates.

Interpretation:

Math poses greater challenges to students, possibly due to its abstract and cumulative nature.

Stronger results in Reading and Writing suggest students are more adept at language-based skills, which may align with teaching strategies or the curriculum's focus.

6.3. Percentage Scores

Finding:

Students' percentages, calculated from their total scores, reveal that most students score in the 60–80% range.

A significant number of students barely cross or fail to meet the passing threshold (40%).

Interpretation:

The majority of students perform at a satisfactory level, but those below the passing mark need immediate intervention.

Ceiling percentages reveal a slight optimistic skew in the data, highlighting the importance of nuanced grading.

6.4. Failure across Subjects

Finding:

Students failing in one subject are more likely to fail overall due to compounding challenges.

Failing rates are particularly high in subjects with strict grading or more conceptual difficulty, such as Math.

Interpretation:

Addressing weaknesses in one subject can significantly improve overall performance.

Math, being a common failing subject, should be a primary focus for academic improvements.

6.5. Pass/Fail Ratios

Finding:

Pie charts reveal that the pass ratio is higher for Reading and Writing compared to Math.

The fail ratio is small but significant, indicating that not all students are meeting basic competency requirements.

Interpretation:

Language-based skills (Reading, Writing) are more accessible for most students, whereas Math challenges cognitive and analytical abilities.

A small but persistent failure rate suggests systemic issues like resource allocation, teaching methodologies, or student preparedness.

6.6. Comparative Analysis

Finding:

The correlation between subject-specific performances highlights students who excel in all areas and those who struggle universally.

High achievers consistently score well across subjects, while struggling students often exhibit broad performance deficits.

Interpretation:

Top performers benefit from strong foundational skills and perhaps external support, while struggling students require targeted interventions.

This disparity points to a potential equity gap in educational resources and support systems.

Recommendations

Math-Specific Focus:

Introduce engaging, interactive, and application-based learning resources for Math.

Organize remedial classes and peer mentoring programs for students struggling with Math.

Targeted Support:

Identify students consistently failing across subjects for additional support, including tutoring and personalized learning plans.

Reward Systems:

Acknowledge high achievers through awards or opportunities for advanced programs to maintain motivation.

Curriculum Reforms:

Review and align the curriculum to ensure it caters to a diverse range of learners and their capabilities.

Student Engagement:

Incorporate extracurricular activities and alternative teaching methods to create a more engaging learning environment.

Parental Involvement:

Share performance insights with parents to align support structures at home and school.

```
In [39]: # Checking which student has failed in overall

         data['status'] = data.apply( lambda x: 'fail' if x['pass_math'] == 'fail' or x['pass_reading'] == 'fail'
                                     or x['pass_writing'] == 'Fail' else 'pass', axis = 1)

         data['status'].value_counts(dropna = True).plot.bar(color = 'gray', figsize = (15, 5))

         plt.title('Overall results')
         plt.xlabel('Status')
         plt.ylabel('count')
         plt.show()
```

Fig 6.1: Code to visualise the status of Pass and Fail students

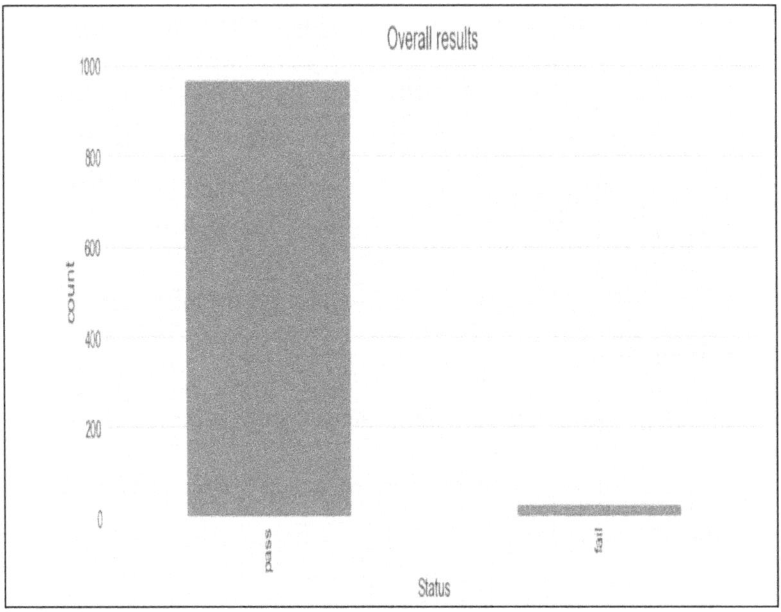

Fig 6.2: To visualise the status of Pass and Fail students

The above code is intended to check if any student has failed in one or more subjects (math, reading, or writing) and then determine their overall status as either fail or pass. Below is a detailed breakdown of the process:

Observations

Logic for Failing Status:

A student is marked as 'fail' if they fail in any one of the three subjects (pass_math, pass_reading, or pass_writing).

Lambda function is used within to compute the status row by row.

Bar Plot for Results:

The count of students in each category (pass or fail) is visualized as a bar chart.

6.7. Hypotheses in Student Performance Analysis

Formulating hypotheses helps establish assumptions about student performance, which can then be tested using statistical analysis or further investigation [42][43]. Here are some key hypotheses related to student performance in exams:

6.7.1. Hypothesis 1: Gender-based differences in cognitive development

Societal expectations may influence subject-specific performance.

Testing: To check which gender has a better performance in the different subjects.

First we are going to do is create a new function because we are going to use the same code, so to avoid repeat code we create a function to create new graphs.

```
def create_graph(group):
  import matplotlib.pyplot as plt
  import seaborn as sns
  fig, ax = plt.subplots()
  fig.subplots_adjust(hspace=0.8, wspace=0.8, left = 0.2, right = 1.5)
  for idx in range(3):
      plt.subplot(1, 3, idx+1)
      gender_df = data.groupby(group)[list(data.columns[-
3:])[idx]].describe()
      ax = sns.barplot(gender_df.index, gender_df.loc[:,"mean"].values)
      plt.ylabel("score")
      plt.title(list(data.columns[-3:])[idx])
      for p in ax.patches:
        ax.annotate('{:.1f}'.format(p.get_height()),(p.get_x()+0.2,
p.get_height()-10))
  plt.show()
```

Now we can create the graph to answer the question.

```
create_graph('gender')
```

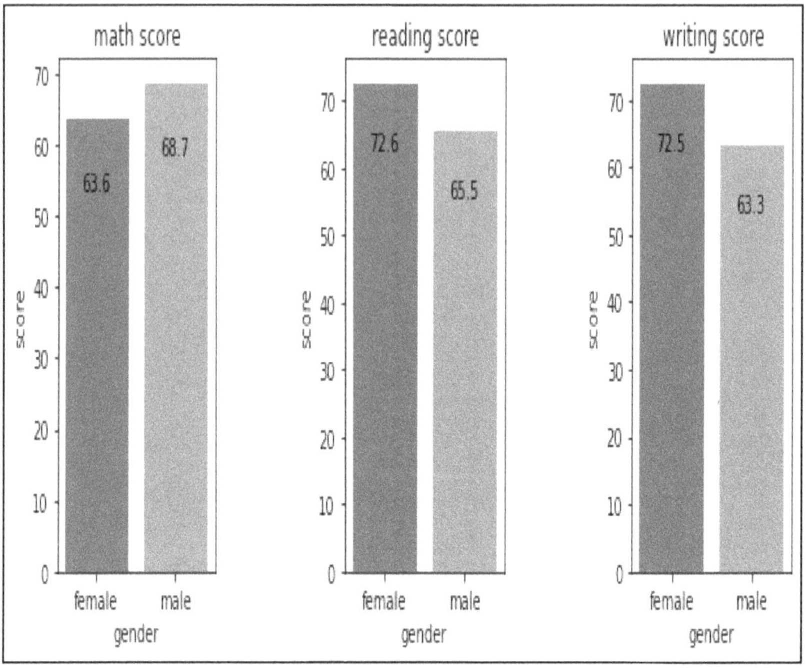

Fig 6.3: To display bar graph to visualise gender wise of reading, writing and math score

With the above reading we can see that the men are better at math but in reading and writing women are better. The other variable we have is the preparations test, and we want to know if the students that take this preparation course affect the exam grade.

6.7.2. Hypothesis 2: Performance of students on the basis of parental education.

The performance of the students is better if the parents has a better level of education.

We can note that if the education of the parents impact the performance in the exams of the students and how much this impact.

Code:

```
parental_education = data.pivot_table(
index=['parental level of education'],
values=['math score', 'reading score', 'writing score'],
aggfunc=np.mean )
display(parental_education)
parental_education.nlargest(1, ['math score', 'reading score', 'writing score'])
```

parental level of education	math score	reading score	writing score
associate's degree	67.882883	70.927928	69.896396
bachelor's degree	69.389831	73.000000	73.381356
high school	62.137755	64.704082	62.448980
master's degree	69.745763	75.372881	75.677966
some college	67.128319	69.460177	68.840708
some high school	63.497207	66.938547	64.888268

parental level of education	math score	reading score	writing score
master's degree	69.745763	75.372881	75.677966

Table 6.1: To show the table of math, reading and writing score as per parental wise education

Students with parents that has a master's degree has a better performance, but in a graph we can see better the information.

```
fig, ax = plt.subplots()
```

```
ax.plot(
    parental_education.index,
    parental_education['math score'],
    marker='o'
    )
ax.plot(
    parental_education.index,
    parental_education['reading score'],
    marker='o'    )
ax.plot(
    parental_education.index,
    parental_education['writing score'],
    marker='o'    )
ax.legend(['Math', 'Reading', 'Writing'])
plt.xticks(rotation=90)
plt.show()
```

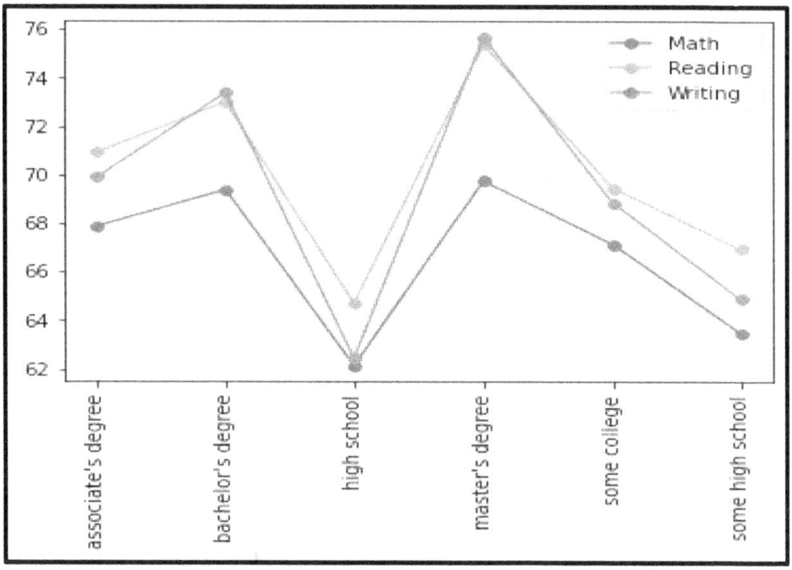

Fig 6.4: To visualise through line graph to show math. Reading and writing score as according to parental level of education

We can see that students with parents who have a master's degree have a better performance in the exams than those students with other education. But in math, the students with parents in bachelor's degree and master's degree has the same grade.

Students with parents with high school education has the worse performance.

6.7.3. Hypothesis 3: To find out with which race/ethnicity has the better performance in the exams.

```
pivot_race = data.pivot_table(index=['race/ethnicity'],
                              values=['math score', 'reading score', 'writing score'],
                              aggfunc=np.mean)
```

display(pivot_race)

race/ethnicity	math score	reading score	writing score
group A	61.629213	64.674157	62.674157
group B	63.452632	67.352632	65.600000
group C	64.463950	69.103448	67.827586
group D	67.362595	70.030534	70.145038
group E	73.821429	73.028571	71.407143

Table 6.2:To display the record of math , reading and writing score as per Race/ethnicity

In the above table, the mean of the exam grades by every race.

pivot_race.nlargest(1, ['math score', 'reading score', 'writing score'])

race/ethnicity	math score	reading score	writing score
group E	73.821429	73.028571	71.407143

Table 6.3: The group E is the group with the best performance during the exams

Code to find out the gender and race/ethnicity with the better performance in the exams

```
pivot_gender_race = data.pivot_table(
  index=['gender', 'race/ethnicity'],
  values=['math score', 'reading score', 'writing score'],
  aggfunc=np.mean )
display(pivot_gender_race)
```

		math score	reading score	writing score
gender	race/ethnicity			
female	group A	58.527778	69.000000	67.861111
	group B	61.403846	71.076923	70.048077
	group C	62.033333	71.944444	71.777778
	group D	65.248062	74.046512	75.023256
	group E	70.811594	75.840580	75.536232
male	group A	63.735849	61.735849	59.150943
	group B	65.930233	62.848837	60.220930
	group C	67.611511	65.424460	62.712230
	group D	69.413534	66.135338	65.413534
	group E	76.746479	70.295775	67.394366

Table 6.4: To display the record of math, reading and writing score as per Race/ethnicity and gender wise

```
pivot_gender_race.nlargest(2, ['math score', 'reading score', 'writing score'])
```

gender	race/ethnicity	math score	reading score	writing score
male	group E	76.746479	70.295775	67.394366
female	group E	70.811594	75.840580	75.536232

Table 6.5: Table to display the group E in both gender has the better performance during the exams.

Now we want to make graphs to see this data.

Code:

```
pivot_gender_race = pivot_gender_race.reset_index()

pivot_gender_female = pivot_gender_race[pivot_gender_race['gender'] == 'female']

fig, ax = plt.subplots()

ax.plot(

   pivot_gender_female['race/ethnicity'],

   pivot_gender_female['math score'],

   marker='o'   )

ax.plot(

   pivot_gender_female['race/ethnicity'],

   pivot_gender_female['reading score'],

   marker='o'  )
```

```
ax.plot(
    pivot_gender_female['race/ethnicity'],
    pivot_gender_female['writing score'],
    marker='o'    )
ax.legend(['Math', 'Reading', 'Writing'])
ax.set_title('Female')
plt.xticks(rotation=90)
plt.show()
```

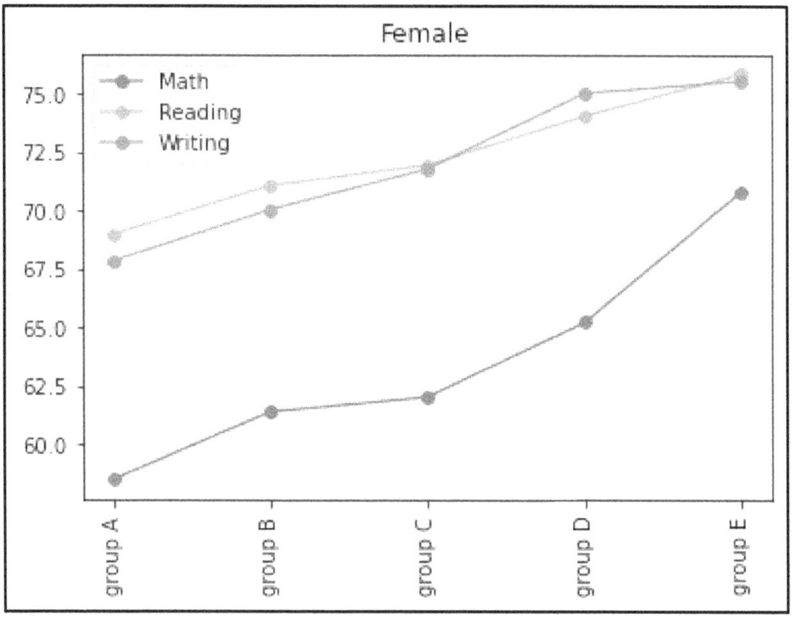

Fig 6.5:To visualise the mean of exam grades of the women in each group.

Here we can see

Code:

```
pivot_gender_male = pivot_gender_race[pivot_gender_race['gender'] ==
'male']

fig, ax = plt.subplots()

ax.plot(
    pivot_gender_male['race/ethnicity'],
    pivot_gender_male['math score'],
    marker='o'    )

ax.plot(
    pivot_gender_male['race/ethnicity'],
    pivot_gender_male['reading score'],
    marker='o'    )

ax.plot(
    pivot_gender_male['race/ethnicity'],
    pivot_gender_male['writing score'],
    marker='o'    )

ax.legend(['Math', 'Reading', 'Writing'])

ax.set_title('Male')

plt.show()
```

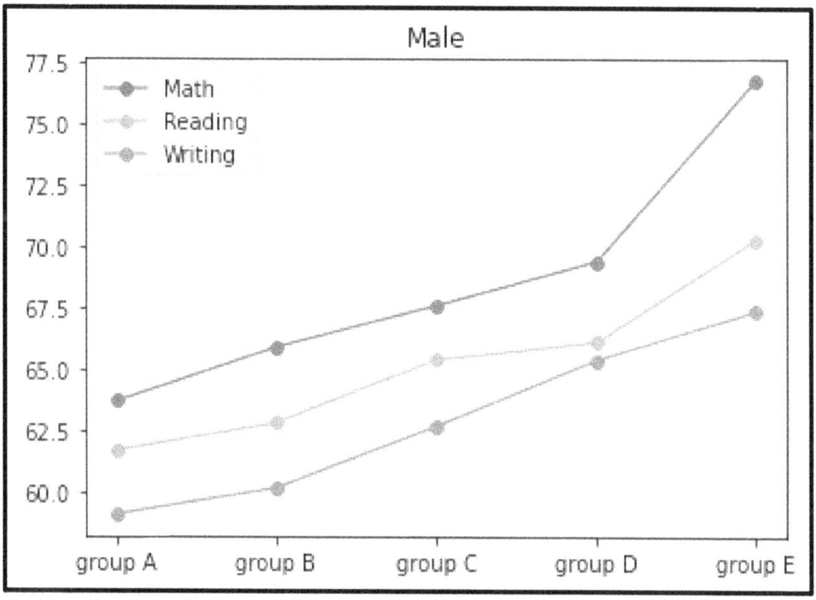

Fig 6.6:To visualise the mean of exam grades of the men in each group.

Here we can see the mean of exam grades of the men in each group.

Code:

```
fig, ax = plt.subplots(3, 1, sharex=True, figsize=(15,10))
ax[0].plot(
    pivot_gender_female['race/ethnicity'],
    pivot_gender_female['math score'],
    marker='o'
    )
ax[0].plot(
    pivot_gender_male['race/ethnicity'],
    pivot_gender_male['math score'],
```

```
    marker='o'
  )
  ax[1].plot(
    pivot_gender_female['race/ethnicity'],
    pivot_gender_female['reading score'],
    marker='o'
  )
  ax[1].plot(
    pivot_gender_male['race/ethnicity'],
    pivot_gender_male['reading score'],
    marker='o'
  )
  ax[2].plot(
    pivot_gender_female['race/ethnicity'],
    pivot_gender_female['writing score'],
    marker='o'
  )
  ax[2].plot(
    pivot_gender_male['race/ethnicity'],
    pivot_gender_male['writing score'],
```

```
    marker='o'
    )
ax[0].legend(['Female', 'Male'])
ax[0].title.set_text('Math Score')
ax[1].title.set_text('Reading Score')
ax[2].title.set_text('Writing Score')
plt.show()
```

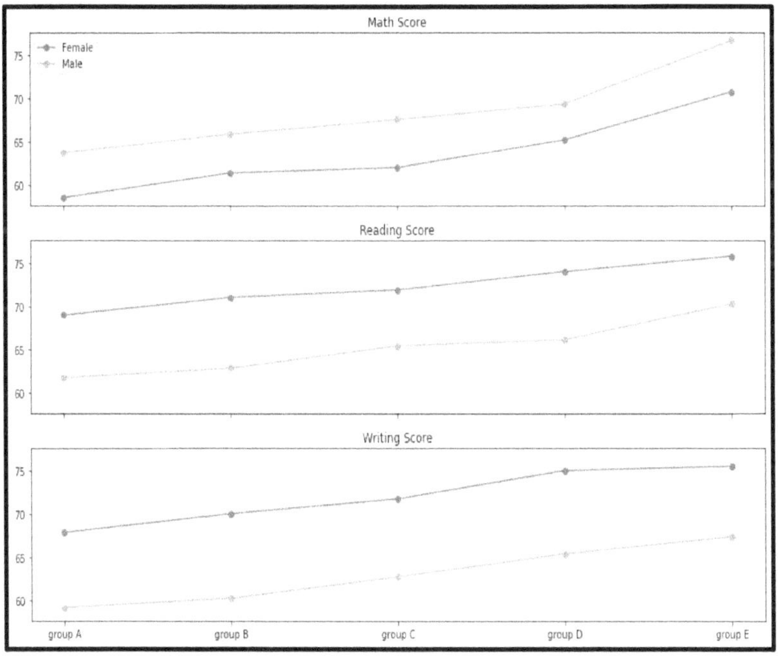

Fig 6.7: To visualise through line graph to take the reading of the math, reading and writing score of different race/ethnicity group gender wise

6.7.4. Conclusion of the Hypothesis

At the end, we can say that the performance is affected by things like take a preparation course or the parent's studies, this can be because if the parents have better studies they can help to their children with their studies [44].

Finally, seems to be that the men are better for mathematics and women better for reading and writing, and the GROUP E in the race/ethnicity is the group with the best average score.

```
In [40]: # Setting a passing marks for the Students to Pass on the three subject individually
         passmarks = 40
         plt.rcParams['figure.figsize'] = (18, 12)

         # Creating a new column pass_math,this column will tell us whether the students are Pass or Fail

         data['pass_math'] = np.where(data['math score']< passmarks, 'Fail', 'Pass')
         data['pass_reading'] = np.where(data['reading score']< passmarks, 'Fail', 'Pass')
         data['pass_writing'] = np.where(data['writing score']< passmarks, 'Fail', 'Pass')

         # Pie chart to represent the ratio of Pass and Fail Status between the students

         size = data['pass_math'].value_counts()
         colors = plt.cm.Reds(np.linspace(0, 1, 3))
         labels = "pass", "fail"
         explode = [0, 0.2]

         plt.subplot(1, 3, 1)
         plt.pie(size, colors = colors, labels = labels, autopct = '%.2f%%', explode = explode, shadow= True)
         plt.title('Student Result For Maths', fontsize = 20)
         plt.legend()

         size = data['pass_reading'].value_counts()
         colors = plt.cm.Reds(np.linspace(0, 1, 2))
         labels = "pass", "fail"
         explode = [0, 0.2]

         plt.subplot(1, 3, 2)
         plt.pie(size, colors = colors, labels = labels, autopct = '%.2f%%', explode = explode, shadow= True)
         plt.title('Student Result For Reading', fontsize = 20)
         plt.legend()
```

Fig 6.8: Code to visualise through Pie Chart to see all students Math, Reading and Writing score.

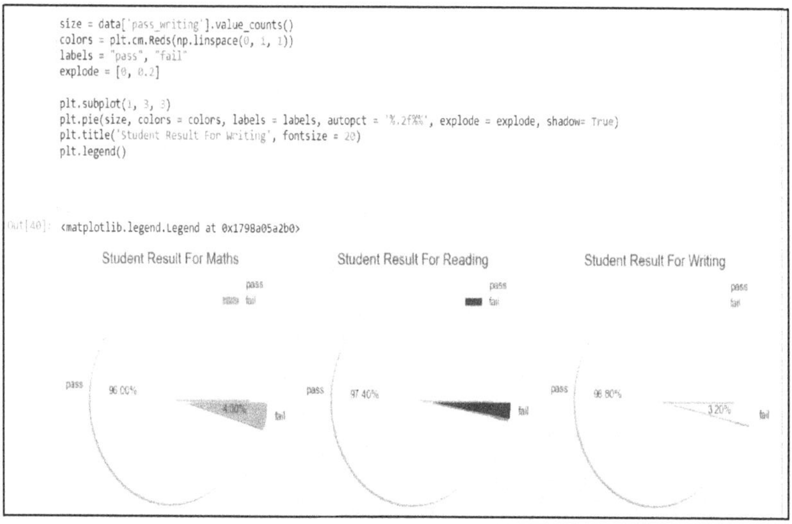

Fig 6.9: Visualise through Pie Chart to see all students Math, Reading and Writing score.

The above code creates a pie chart for each subject to visualize the proportion of students passing or failing, based on a defined pass marks threshold. Here are some observations:

6.8. Setting Passing Marks:

6.8.1. Observation

The passmarks is = 40 and use np.where to determine whether students passed or failed in each subject. The new columns (pass_math, pass_reading, and pass_writing) store the results as 'Pass' or 'Fail'.

Pie Charts for Pass/Fail Ratios:

Separate pie charts are created for math, reading, and writing, displaying the proportion of students who passed or failed.

Customizations:

Each pie chart has its own title, legend, and explosion effect for the 'Fail' segment.

The pie chart code is repeated for each subject, which could be simplified using a loop for efficiency and clarity.

Uniform Labels:

"pass", "fail" labels are static, assuming the same pass/fail status exists for all subjects. These labels should dynamically adapt to the data.

Outcome

The code creates:

Three pie charts showing the proportion of students who passed and failed in math, reading, and writing.

Each chart uses shades of red, includes percentages, and highlights "Fail" with an offset for emphasis.

```
jupyter StudentPerformanceAnalysis-Copy1 Last Checkpoint: Last Tuesday at 2:12 AM (autosaved)

In [36]: # Assigning grades to the grades according to the following criteria:
         # 0 - 40 Marks : Grade E
         # 41 - 60 Marks : Grade D
         # 60 - 70 Marks : Grade C
         # 70 - 80 Marks : Grade B
         # 80 - 90 Marks : Grade A
         # 90 - 100 Marks : Grade O

         def getgrade(percentage, status):
             if status == 'fail':
                 return 'E'
             if percentage >= 90:
                 return 'O'  # Assuming "O" is correct as per criteria
             if percentage >= 80:
                 return 'A'
             if percentage >= 70:
                 return 'B'
             if percentage >= 60:
                 return 'C'
             if percentage >= 41:
                 return 'D'
             else:
                 return 'E'

         # Applying the function
         data['grades'] = data.apply(lambda x: getgrade(x['percentage'], x['status']), axis=1)
         print(data['grades'].value_counts())
```

Fig 6.10: Code to set the Grade as per Final Marks of all students.

```
B    260
C    252
D    239
A    156
O     58
E     35
Name: grades, dtype: int64
```

Fig 6.11: Output of the code to set the Grade as per Final Marks of all students(1000).

Here's a breakdown of the code

6.9. Assigns grades based on student marks and status:

Adding a Comment

Code

```
# Assigning grades according to the following criteria:

# 0 - 40 Marks : Grade E

# 41 - 60 Marks : Grade D

# 60 - 70 Marks : Grade C

# 70 - 80 Marks : Grade B

# 80 - 90 Marks : Grade A

# 90 - 100 Marks : Grade 0
```

Explanation : This comment explains the grading criteria based on percentage marks. Students are assigned grades from 'E' (lowest) to '0' (highest).

Defining the Grading Function

Code

```
def getgrade(percentage, status):

   if status == 'fail':

      return 'E'

   if percentage >= 90:

      return '0'  # Assuming '0' is correct based on the criteria

   if percentage >= 80:
```

```
        return 'A'
    if percentage >= 70:
        return 'B'
    if percentage >= 60:
        return 'C'
    if percentage >= 41:
        return 'D'
    else:
        return 'E'
```

How This Code Works:

Inputs:

percentage: Marks obtained by the student.

status: Whether the student passed or failed.

Logic Flow:

If the student's status is 'fail', they get an automatic grade of 'E', regardless of marks.

If percentage >= 90, grade '0' is assigned (assuming '0' is intentional, not 'O').

Subsequent checks assign corresponding grades based on the percentage ranges.

The else ensures students scoring 0-40 receive grade 'E'.

6.10. Applying the Function to the Dataframe

Code & its Explanation

data['grades'] = data.apply(lambda x: getgrade(x['percentage'], x['status']), axis=1)

data.apply(): Applies the getgrade function row by row to the dataframe data.

lambda x:: A short anonymous function that passes each row x to the getgrade function using its percentage and status columns.

axis=1: Ensures row-wise operation.

data['grades']: Stores the calculated grades in a new column grades in the dataframe.

6.11. Counting and Displaying Grade Distribution

Code & its Explanation

print(data['grades'].value_counts())

data['grades'].value_counts(): Counts occurrences of each grade in the grades column.

print(): Displays the count of each grade in the console/output window.

Key Notes:

Consistency Check: Verify that grade '0' is intended (not 'O').

Data Requirement: Ensure that data is defined as a dataframe with columns percentage and status before running the code.

Logical Flow: The function checks conditions in descending order, ensuring the correct grade assignment.

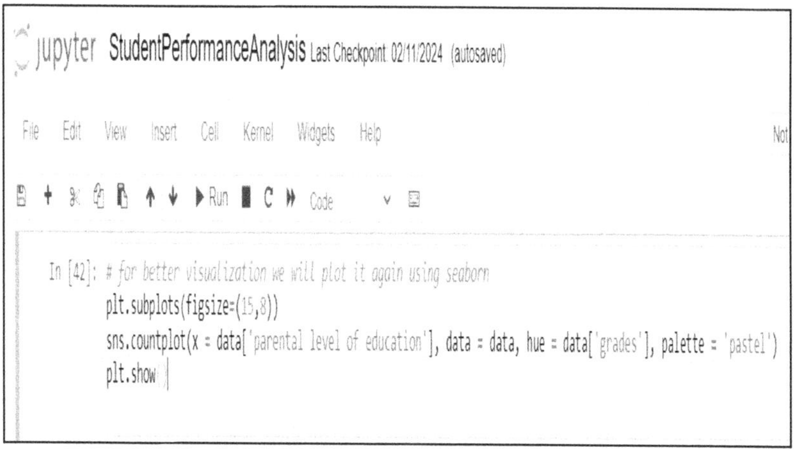

Fig 6.12:Code to visualise the grade of students as according to their parental level of education.

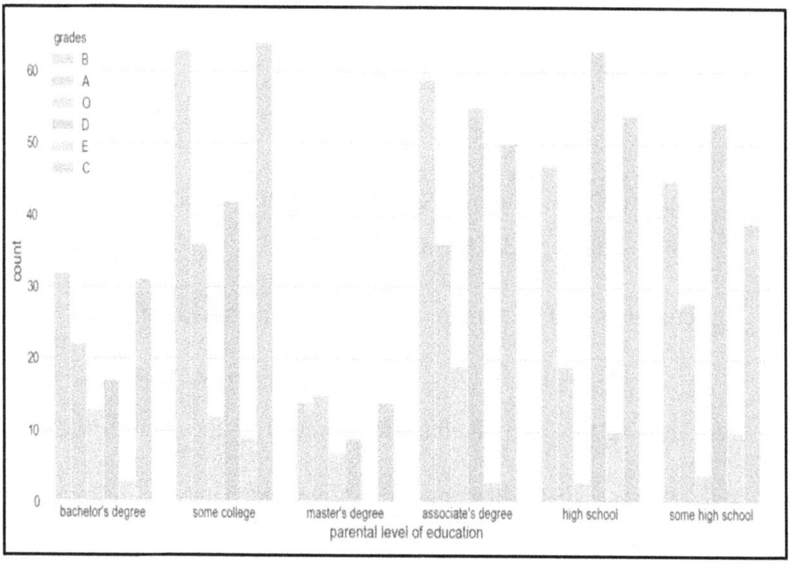

Fig 6.13: Display Bar Graph to visualise the grade of students as according to their parental level of education.

1. Adding a Comment

Code

 # for better visualization we will plot it again using seaborn

Explanation: This comment explains the purpose of the following code: visualizing data with Seaborn for better readability and aesthetics.

2. Setting the Figure Size

Code

plt.subplots(figsize=(15, 8))

Explanation: This line creates a new figure with a specified size of 15 inches wide and 8 inches tall.

plt.subplots() returns two objects: a figure and axes. However, since the axes object isn't needed here, it's ignored.

Creating the Count Plot

Code

Explanation:sns.countplot(x = data['parental level of education'], data = data, hue = data['grades'], palette = 'pastel')

sns.countplot(): This function creates a count-based bar plot.

x = data['parental level of education']: This specifies the x-axis, representing the parental education levels from the dataframe data.

data = data: Specifies the dataframe from which the data is sourced (though it is redundant here because the x is already provided).

hue = data['grades']: This breaks down the count bars by the grades column, showing different grades using separate colors.

palette = 'pastel': This sets the bar colors to a soft pastel color scheme for better aesthetics.

Displaying the Plot

Code

plt.show()

Explanation: This command displays the plot in the output window.

Overall Purpose:

The code visualizes how grades are distributed across different levels of parental education. The bars are grouped by grades, allowing easy comparison. Each grade is represented by a different pastel color, enhancing readability and visual appeal.

```
In [38]: # Comparing the distribution of grades among males and females
         plt.subplots(figsize=(15,8))
         sns.countplot(x = data['grades'], data = data, hue = data['gender'], palette = 'cubehelix')
         plt.show()
```

Fig 6.14: Code to visualise the grade of students as according to their gender wise.

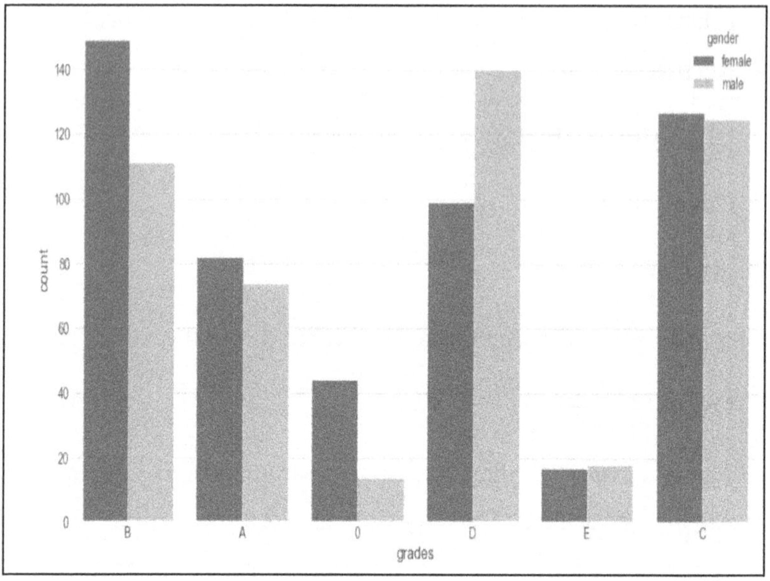

Fig 6.15: Display Bar Graph to visualise the grade of students as according to their gender wise.

Here's a detailed explanation of the code that compares the distribution of grades among males and females using Seaborn and Matplotlib:

- **Adding a Comment**

  Code

  # Comparing the distribution of grades among males and females

  Explanation: This comment explains the purpose of the plot: to compare how grades are distributed between male and female students.

- **Setting the Figure Size**

  Code

```
plt.subplots(figsize=(15,8))
```

plt.subplots(figsize=(15, 8)):

Explanation: This creates a figure with dimensions of 15 inches wide and 8 inches tall. A larger figure size makes the plot more readable, especially when dealing with a lot of data.

- **Creating the Count Plot**

Code

```
sns.countplot(x=data['grades'],data=data,hue=data['gender'],
palette='cubehelix')
```

sns.countplot(): This function creates a count-based bar plot, showing how frequently each grade occurs.

Parameters Explained:

x=data['grades']: Specifies the x-axis, showing different grades ('A', 'B', 'C', etc.).

data=data: Specifies the dataframe data as the source of the data.

hue=data['gender']: Separates each bar by gender, creating sub-bars within each grade.

palette='cubehelix': Sets the color scheme to Seaborn's cubehelix palette, which uses a visually distinct color gradient.

- **Displaying the Plot**

Code

```
plt.show()
```

plt.show():

Explanation: Displays the generated plot. Without this, the plot won't appear in most environments.

Overall Purpose

The code visualizes how grades are distributed among male and female students. Each grade category has two sub-bars: one for males and one for females. This comparison helps identify trends such as whether one gender outperforms the other in specific grades.

6.12. Creating Heat map to show the correlation between the attributes

```
In [39]: # heatmap

         plt.rcParams['figure.figsize'] = (18,6)
         sns.heatmap(data.corr(), cmap = 'rainbow', annot=True)
         plt.title('Correlations between the attributes', fontsize = 20)
```

Fig 6.16: Code to generate Heatmap to visualize correlation between attributes in a Data Frame

Out[39]: Text(0.5, 1.0, 'Correlations between the attributes')

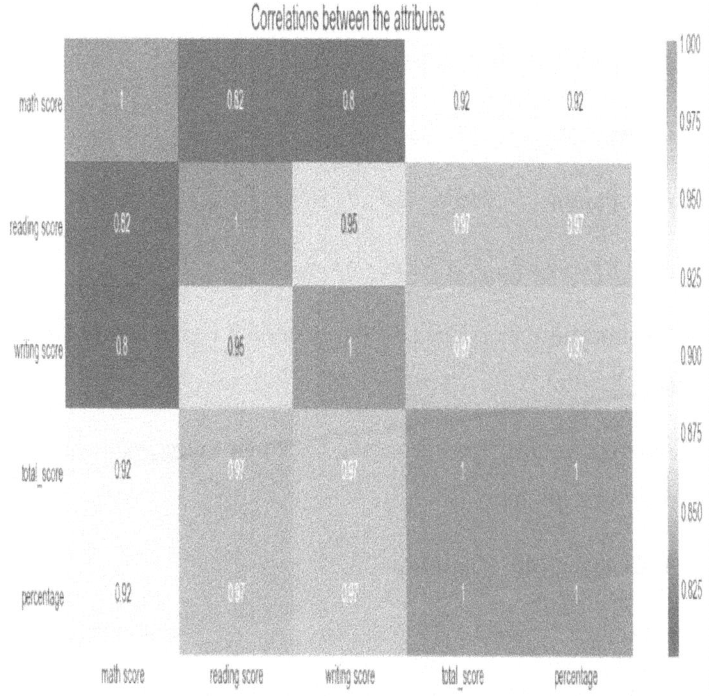

Fig 6.17: Generate Heatmap to visualize correlation between attributes in a Data Frame

Here's a detailed explanation of the code that generates a heatmap to visualize correlations between attributes in a Dataframe using Seaborn and Matplotlib:

1. Adding a Comment

Python

Code

 # heatmap

Explanation

This comment indicates that a Heatmap visualization will be generated.

2. Setting the Figure Size

Code

plt.rcParams['figure.figsize'] = (18,6)

plt.rcParams['figure.figsize'] = (18,6):

Explanation: This line adjusts the default figure size to 18 inches wide and 6 inches tall.

A larger figure size makes the Heatmap more readable, especially when dealing with many features.

3. Creating the Heatmap

Code

sns.heatmap(data.corr(), cmap='rainbow', annot=True)

Explanation:

sns.heatmap(): This function generates a Heatmap from a 2D data array.

Key Parameters Explained:

data.corr(): Calculates the correlation matrix of numerical columns in the dataframe data. This matrix shows the strength and direction of relationships between features (values between -1 and 1).

cmap='rainbow': Sets the Heatmap color scheme to a rainbow gradient, where colors represent the degree of correlation.

annot=True: Displays the correlation values inside the Heatmap cells.

4. Adding a Title

Code

plt.title('Correlations between the attributes', fontsize=20)

plt.title(): Adds a title to the plot for context.

fontsize=20: Sets the font size of the title to make it more visible.

Overall Purpose:

The code generates a heatmap showing how strongly the attributes in the dataframe data are correlated with one another. Strong positive correlations are closer to 1, while strong negative correlations are closer to -1. This helps identify relationships, multicollinearity, and potential predictive features.

```
In [48]: from sklearn.preprocessing import LabelEncoder

         # creating and encoder

         le = LabelEncoder()

         # label encoding for test preparation course

         data['test preparation course'] = le.fit_transform(data['test preparation course'])

         #label encoding for lunch

         data['lunch'] = le.fit_transform(data['lunch'])
```

Fig 6.18: This code performs label encoding on two categorical columns (test preparation course and lunch) in a dataset.

Label encoding is a technique used to convert categorical variables into numerical values, making them suitable for machine learning algorithms that require numerical input.

Here's a detailed explanation of the code:

Step-by-Step Breakdown:

Importing LabelEncoder:

Code

```
from sklearn.preprocessing import LabelEncoder
```

Explanation: This imports the LabelEncoder class from the sklearn.preprocessing module. LabelEncoder is a utility provided by scikit-learn for encoding categorical variables as integers.

Creating an Encoder:

Code

```
le = LabelEncoder()
```

Explanation: This initializes a LabelEncoder object called le. This object will be used to convert the categorical data into numerical values.

Label Encoding for "test preparation course":

Code

```
data['test preparation course'] = le.fit_transform(data['test preparation course'])
```

Explanation: This line encodes the test preparation course column in the data Dataframe.

fit_transform is a combination of two functions:

fit: It analyzes the unique values in the test preparation course column (i.e., it learns the unique categories).

transform: It converts each unique category into a numerical label (i.e., assigns an integer to each category).

The result is stored back in the test preparation course column, where each category (e.g., "completed", "none") is replaced by an integer.

Label Encoding for "lunch":

Code

```
data['lunch'] = le.fit_transform(data['lunch'])
```

Explanation: This line performs label encoding for the lunch column, following the same process as with the test preparation course column.

It transforms categorical values in the lunch column (e.g., "standard", "free") into numerical labels.

The encoded values are stored back in the lunch column.

Assume the original columns have the following categorical values:

test preparation course: ["completed", "none", "completed", "none"]

lunch: ["standard", "free", "standard", "free"]

After applying LabelEncoder, the columns will be transformed into numerical values like this:

test preparation course: [1, 0, 1, 0] (where "completed" = 1, "none" = 0)

lunch: [1, 0, 1, 0] (where "standard" = 1, "free" = 0)

Overall:

6.13. Converting categorical values to numerical using Label Encoder

The code converts the categorical values in the test preparation course and lunch columns into numerical labels using Label Encoder. This is a common preprocessing step in machine learning to make categorical data compatible with algorithms that require numeric input [47][48].

```
In [41]: # label encoding for race/ethnicity
         # we have to map values to each of the categories

         data['race/ethnicity'] = data['race/ethnicity'].replace('group A', 1)
         data['race/ethnicity'] = data['race/ethnicity'].replace('group B', 2)
         data['race/ethnicity'] = data['race/ethnicity'].replace('group C', 3)
         data['race/ethnicity'] = data['race/ethnicity'].replace('group D', 4)
         data['race/ethnicity'] = data['race/ethnicity'].replace('group E', 5)

         data['race/ethnicity'].value_counts()

Out[41]: 3    319
         4    262
         2    190
         5    140
         1     89
         Name: race/ethnicity, dtype: int64
```

Fig 6.19: This code performs manual label encoding for the categorical column race/ethnicity in the data Dataframe. Instead of using the LabelEncoder from scikit-learn, the code uses the replace () method to map each category to a numerical value directly.

Step-by-Step Breakdown:

Label Encoding for race/ethnicity:

Code

data['race/ethnicity'] = data['race/ethnicity'].replace('group A', 1)

data['race/ethnicity'] = data['race/ethnicity'].replace('group B', 2)

data['race/ethnicity'] = data['race/ethnicity'].replace('group C', 3)

```
data['race/ethnicity'] = data['race/ethnicity'].replace('group D', 4)

data['race/ethnicity'] = data['race/ethnicity'].replace('group E', 5)
```

Explanation: These lines replace each category in the race/ethnicity column with an integer.

The replace() function is applied to the data['race/ethnicity'] column in each line to replace the corresponding category ("group A", "group B", etc.) with a numerical value.

'group A' is replaced with 1

'group B' is replaced with 2

'group C' is replaced with 3

'group D' is replaced with 4

'group E' is replaced with 5

This manually maps each of the race/ethnicity groups to a corresponding integer value.

Count of Unique Values (Post-Encoding):

Code

```
data['race/ethnicity'].value_counts()
```

Explanation: This line calculates and displays the count of each unique value in the race/ethnicity column after the encoding.

The value_counts() method returns the number of occurrences of each unique value (i.e., how many times each group appears after replacing categories with integers).

Overall:

This code replaces categorical values in the race/ethnicity column with numerical labels manually.

It then counts the occurrences of each encoded value using value_counts(), which helps you understand how many times each category (now encoded as integers) appears in the dataset.

```
In [42]: # level encoding for parental level of education

         data['parental level of education'] = le.fit_transform(data['parental level of education'])

         data['parental level of education'].value_counts()

Out[42]: 4    226
         0    222
         2    196
         5    179
         1    118
         3     59
         Name: parental level of education, dtype: int64
```

Fig- 6.20 -This code performs label encoding on the parental level of education column in the data Dataframe using LabelEncoder from scikit-learn.

Here's a detailed breakdown:

Step-by-Step Breakdown:

Label Encoding for parental level of education:

Code

data['parental level of education'] = le.fit_transform(data['parental level of education'])

le.fit_transform():

Explanation : This is a combination of two methods:

fit(): Analyzes the unique values in the parental level of education column (e.g., "high school", "associate's degree", etc.), and assigns an integer value to each unique category.

transform(): Converts the categories in the parental level of education column to their corresponding numerical values.

The transformed values (integers) are then assigned back to the parental level of education column. For example:

"high school" might be encoded as 0

"associate's degree" as 1

"some college" as 2, and so on.

LabelEncoder encodes the categorical variable into an ordered list of integers.

Counting Encoded Values:

Code

data['parental level of education'].value_counts()

value_counts(): This function counts how many times each unique value (now an integer) appears in the parental level of education column after label encoding.

The result shows how many times each encoded level of parental education occurs in the dataset, helping to verify the distribution of categories.

Overall:

This code uses label encoding to transform the categorical data in the parental level of education column into numerical values.

It then counts the occurrences of each encoded value to show the distribution of different education levels in the dataset.

```
In [43]: # label encoding for gender

         data['gender'] = le.fit_transform(data['gender'])

         # label encoding for math

         data['pass_math'] = le.fit_transform(data['pass_math'])

         # label encoding for reading

         data['pass_reading'] = le.fit_transform(data['pass_reading'])

         # label encoding for writing

         data['pass_writing'] = le.fit_transform(data['pass_writing'])

         # label encoding for status

         data['status'] = le.fit_transform(data['status'])
```

Fig-6.21-This code performs label encoding on multiple categorical columns in the data Dataframe. Label encoding is a technique used to convert categorical data into numerical values, which is often required for machine learning models. The LabelEncoder from scikit-learn is used to transform the categorical variables into numerical labels.

Here's a breakdown of the code:

1. Label Encoding for gender:

Code:

data['gender'] = le.fit_transform(data['gender'])

Explanation : The gender column contains categorical data (e.g., "male", "female").

le.fit_transform(data['gender']):

fit(): Identifies the unique values in the gender column (e.g., "male", "female") and assigns an integer to each unique value.

transform(): Converts each instance in the gender column to its corresponding integer label.

The resulting numeric values replace the original categorical values in the gender column.

After encoding:

"male" might become 0

"female" might become 1 (depending on the order of appearance)

2. Label Encoding for pass_math:

Code

data['pass_math'] = le.fit_transform(data['pass_math'])

Explanation: The pass_math column contains categorical values (e.g., "yes", "no") indicating whether a student passed the math exam.

The fit_transform function encodes these categorical values into numeric values (e.g., "yes" becomes 1, "no" becomes 0).

3. Label Encoding for pass_reading:

Python

Code

```
data['pass_reading'] = le.fit_transform(data['pass_reading'])
```

Explanation: Similar to pass_math, this encodes the pass_reading column, which may contain values like "yes" or "no", indicating whether a student passed the reading exam.

After encoding, "yes" becomes 1 and "no" becomes 0 (or the reverse, depending on the order encountered by the LabelEncoder).

4. Label Encoding for pass_writing:

Code

```
data['pass_writing'] = le.fit_transform(data['pass_writing'])
```

Explanation: This line encodes the pass_writing column, which contains categorical values such as "yes" and "no" (indicating if a student passed the writing exam).

The encoding is similar to the previous steps, converting categorical values into numerical labels.

5. Label Encoding for status:

Code

```
data['status'] = le.fit_transform(data['status'])
```

Explanation: The status column likely indicates a student's status, such as "completed" or "not completed".

After encoding, categorical values in the status column are replaced by integers (e.g., "completed" could be 1, "not completed" could be 0).

Summary of the Process:

fit_transform() is used to learn and then apply the transformation to the categorical data in each column.

The categorical columns (gender, pass_math, pass_reading, pass_writing, and status) are converted into numeric labels so that they can be used as input to machine learning algorithms, which generally require numerical data.

After encoding, the original categorical columns are replaced with their corresponding numeric labels.

```
In [44]: # label encoding for grades
         # We have to map values to ech of the categories

         data['grades'] = data['grades'].replace('O', 0)
         data['grades'] = data['grades'].replace('A', 1)
         data['grades'] = data['grades'].replace('B', 2)
         data['grades'] = data['grades'].replace('C', 3)
         data['grades'] = data['grades'].replace('D', 4)
         data['grades'] = data['grades'].replace('E', 5)

         data['grades'].value_counts()

Out[44]: 2    260
         3    252
         4    239
         1    156
         0     58
         5     35
         Name: grades, dtype: int64
```

6.22:-This code performs manual label encoding on the grades column in the data Dataframe.

The goal is to map the categorical grade values ('O', 'A', 'B', etc.) to numerical values so that they can be used in machine learning models.

Step-by-Step Breakdown:

Manual mapping for grades Column:

Code

```
data['grades'] = data['grades'].replace('O', 0)

data['grades'] = data['grades'].replace('A', 1)

data['grades'] = data['grades'].replace('B', 2)

data['grades'] = data['grades'].replace('C', 3)

data['grades'] = data['grades'].replace('D', 4)

data['grades'] = data['grades'].replace('E', 5)
```

Explanation: The replace() method is used to manually map each grade (which is a categorical value) to a numerical value.

Here's the mapping for the grades:

'O' (Outstanding) → 0

'A' → 1

'B' → 2

'C' → 3

'D' → 4

'E' (Fail) → 5

The replace() method replaces each occurrence of a specific grade (e.g., 'O', 'A') with its corresponding numerical value. This step is repeated for all grades in the grades column.

Counting Encoded Values:

Code

```
data['grades'].value_counts()
```

Explanation: The value_counts() function counts how many times each unique numerical value appears in the grades column after the encoding.

This will return a summary of how many students have received each grade (now represented as a number) in the dataset.

Overall

This code manually encodes the categorical grade values (like 'O', 'A', 'B', etc.) into numerical values.

It uses the replace() method to assign numerical values to each grade.

The value_counts() function then shows the frequency of each encoded grade in the dataset, helping to understand the distribution of grades.

6.14. Data Modelling: Splitting the dependent and independent variables.

Data modeling for student performance analysis in an examination using machine learning involves using machine learning techniques to analyze and predict student performance based on various features such as study habits, attendance, parental education level, and other factors [49].

Model selection in machine learning refers to the process of choosing the most appropriate algorithm or model to solve a given problem based on the characteristics of the dataset and the specific task at hand. The goal is to find a model that generalizes well to unseen data and provides the best performance [50].

The selection of the right model depends on several factors including the type of problem, the nature of the data, and the desired output. Below is an overview of model selection, the considerations involved, and a guide to choosing the right model:

Data modeling for student performance analysis in exams involves building machine learning models that use student-related features (e.g., study time, previous scores, gender, etc.) to predict exam outcomes [51].

The process includes data collection, preprocessing, exploratory data analysis, model training, evaluation, and deployment.

In the context of student performance analysis for an examination using machine learning, splitting the dependent and independent variables refers to separating the features (independent variables) from the target variable (dependent variable) [52]. This step is essential before training a machine learning model, as it allows the model to understand which variables are inputs (features) and which variable is the output (target) that you want to predict.

6.14.1. Understanding the Variables:

Independent Variables (Features or Predictors): These are the variables or columns in the dataset that will be used to make predictions about the target variable [53]. In the case of student performance, independent variables include:

Parental level of education

Previous exam scores (math, reading, writing scores)

Gender

Lunch type (e.g., standard or free/reduced)

Test preparation course (e.g., completed or not)

Social background (e.g., socioeconomic status)

Dependent Variable (Target or Response): This is the variable the model is trying to predict based on the independent variables. In student performance analysis, which is:

Final exam score (regression problem if predicting continuous scores)

Pass/Fail status (classification problem if predicting whether a student passed or failed)

6.14.2. Steps to Split the Variables:

We have a dataset named data that contains various features about students' characteristics and performance.

Here's how you would split the variables into independent and dependent variables:

Data Modeling
Splitting the dependant and independant variables

```
In [ ]:

In [49]: # Splitting the dependant and independant variables

         x = data.iloc[:,:14]
         y = data.iloc[:,14]

         print(x.shape)
         print(y.shape)

         (1000, 14)
         (1000,)
```

Fig-6.23- This code is used in the data preprocessing phase of a machine learning workflow. Its primary purpose is to divide the dataset into independent variables (x) and a dependent variable (y).

Code Breakdown

1. Splitting the Independent (x) and Dependent (y) Variables

Code

x = data.iloc[:, :14]

data.iloc[:, :14]:

iloc: A pandas method used to select rows and columns by integer index.

:: Selects all rows in the dataset.

: 14: Selects columns from index 0 to 13 (first 14 columns, as indexing starts at 0).

Result: x contains the independent variables (features) used to make predictions.

In a student performance dataset, x might include features like "hours studied," "test preparation," and "attendance."

Code

y = data.iloc[:, 14]

data.iloc[:, 14]:

Selects all rows (:).

14: Selects the column at index 14 (the 15th column in zero-based indexing).

Result: y contains the dependent variable (target) that the model will predict.

In a student performance dataset, y might represent the "final exam score" or "pass/fail status."

2. Printing the Shapes

Code

print(x.shape)

print(y.shape)

x.shape:

Returns the dimensions of the independent variable DataFrame x.

Output: (1000, 14) means there are 1000 rows (samples) and 14 columns (features).

y.shape:

Returns the dimensions of the dependent variable Series y.

Output: (1000,) indicates 1000 rows (samples) and no second dimension (as it's a single column).

Purpose of the Code

Independent Variables (x):

These are the features or predictors the model will use to make predictions.

Dependent Variable (y):

This is the target variable the model aims to predict (e.g., a score, grade, or class label).

Shape Validation:

Printing the shapes of x and y ensures that:

The number of rows in x matches the number of rows in y.

The feature matrix (x) has the expected number of columns.

Key Points

This step is crucial for preparing data for machine learning models.

The independent variables (x) are used as input, while the dependent variable (y) is the output the model predicts.

Printing shapes ensures compatibility of data dimensions for further processing (e.g., splitting into train-test sets).

```
In [50]: # Splitting the dataset into training and test sets

         from sklearn.model_selection import train_test_split
         x_train, x_test, y_train, y_test = train_test_split(x, y, test_size=0.25, random_state=45)

         print(x_train.shape)  # Training features
         print(y_train.shape)  # Training target
         print(x_test.shape)   # Test features
         print(y_test.shape)   # Test target

         (750, 14)
         (750,)
         (250, 14)
         (250,)
```

Fig- 6.24: This code is part of the data preparation phase in machine learning, where the dataset is split into training and test sets to evaluate the performance of a model.

Code Breakdown

1. Importing the Function

Code

from sklearn.model_selection import train_test_split

train_test_split:

A function from scikit-learn's model_selection module.

Explanation: It is used to split a dataset into training and test subsets in a random and reproducible way.

6.14.3. Splitting the Dataset

Code

x_train, x_test, y_train, y_test = train_test_split(x, y, test_size=0.25, random_state=45)

Inputs to train_test_split:

x: Independent variables (features).

y: Dependent variable (target).

test_size=0.25:

Specifies that 25% of the data will be used for testing.

The remaining 75% will be used for training.

random_state=45:

Ensures reproducibility by fixing the random seed.

The same split will be generated every time the code runs.

Outputs:

x_train: Training subset of independent variables.

x_test: Test subset of independent variables.

y_train: Training subset of the dependent variable.

y_test: Test subset of the dependent variable.

Printing the Shapes

Code

```
print(x_train.shape)

print(y_train.shape)

print(x_test.shape)
```

print(x_test.shape)

x_train.shape:

Prints the dimensions of the training features.

(750, 14) means 750 rows (samples) and 14 columns (features).

y_train.shape:

Prints the dimensions of the training target.

(750,) means 750 rows (samples) and no second dimension (as it's a single column).

y_test.shape:

Prints the dimensions of the test target.

250, 14) means 250 rows (samples) and 14 columns (features).

Purpose of the Code

6.14.4. Training theDataset:

Used to train the machine learning model (build the relationship between x and y).

Comprises 75% of the data (test_size=0.25 implies 1 - 0.25 = 0.75).

6.14.5. Testing the Dataset:

Used to evaluate the performance of the trained model on unseen data.

Comprises 25% of the data.

Reproducibility:

Setting a random_state ensures consistent results across different runs of the code.

The dataset has:

1000 samples (rows).

14 features (columns).

The output might look like:

plaintext

Copy code

(750, 14) # `x_train`: 750 rows, 14 features

(750,) # `y_train`: 750 rows, 1 target column

(250, 14) # `x_test`: 250 rows, 14 features

(250,) # `y_test`: 250 rows, 1 target column

6.14.6.Summary of creating Model for training and testing data

The training set is used to train the model.

The test set is used to evaluate the model's performance.

Splitting the data ensures the model generalizes well to new, unseen data.

Fixing the random_state makes the results reproducible.

```
In [49]: #import MinMaxScaler
         from sklearn.preprocessing import MinMaxScaler

         # Creating a scaler
         mm = MinMaxScaler()

         # Feeding the Independent Variable into the Scaler
         x_train = mm.fit_transform(x_train)
         x_test = mm.transform(x_test)
```

Fig-6.25-The above code demonstrates how to normalize data using the MinMaxScaler from the scikit-learn library.

Code Explanation:

Importing MinMaxScaler:

from sklearn.preprocessing import MinMaxScaler

The **MinMaxScaler** is a preprocessing tool from scikit-learn used to scale and normalize data to a specific range, typically [0, 1].

6.15. Creating the Scaler:

mm = MinMaxScaler()

Here, an instance of the MinMaxScaler is created and stored in the variable mm.

By default, the scaler transforms values to the range [0, 1], but you can specify a custom range using the feature_range parameter (MinMaxScaler (feature_range=(0, 1))).

Fitting and Transforming the Training Data:

x_train = mm.fit_transform(x_train)

The fit_transform method does two things:

Fits the scaler to the data (x_train), meaning it calculates the minimum and maximum values for each feature in the dataset.

Transforms the data by applying the scaling formula:

Transforming the Test Data:

x_test = mm.transform(x_test)

The transform method applies the scaling (using the same minimum and maximum values calculated from x_train) to the test dataset x_test.

This ensures that the test data is scaled consistently with the training data.

Purpose of Using MinMaxScaler:

Normalize Data: Many machine learning algorithms like gradient-based models, distance-based models like k-NN) perform better when input features have similar scales.

Range Constraint: We have to ensure that all features lie within a specified range, which can improve numerical stability and convergence speed.

6.16. Importing the Random Forest Classifier

```
In [50]: from sklearn.ensemble import RandomForestClassifier

         # Creating a Model
         model = RandomForestClassifier()

         #Feeding the Training Data to the Model
         model.fit(x_train, y_train)

         #Predicting the x_test Results
         y_pred = model.predict(x_test)

         # Calculating the accuracies
         print("Training Accuracy :", model.score(x_train, y_train))
         print("Testing Accuracy :", model.score(x_test, y_test))

         Training Accuracy : 1.0
         Testing Accuracy : 1.0
```

Fig- 6.26: The above code used the RandomForestClassifier from the scikit-learn library for supervised machine learning.

Code Explanation: -

Here's a step-by-step explanation:

Code

from sklearn.ensemble import RandomForestClassifier

The **RandomForestClassifier** is part of the ensemble module in scikit-learn. It is an ensemble learning method that uses multiple decision trees to improve classification accuracy and reduce overfitting.

6.17. Creating the Model

Code

model = RandomForestClassifier()

Here, a Random Forest model is instantiated with the default parameters.

We can customize it by specifying parameters like n_estimators (number of trees), max_depth (depth of trees), and more.

6.18. Training the Model

Code

model.fit(x_train, y_train)

The **.fit()** method is used to train the model using:

x_train: Features (inputs) for training.

y_train: Corresponding labels (outputs).

The model learns patterns from this data.

6.19. Making Predictions

Code

y_pred = model.predict(x_test)

The **.predict()** method is used to make predictions on the test dataset **x_test.**

y_pred contains the predicted labels for **x_test.**

6.20. Calculating Accuracies

Code

print("Training Accuracy :", model.score(x_train, y_train))

print("Testing Accuracy :", model.score(x_test, y_test))

The **.score()** method calculates the accuracy of the model by comparing the predicted labels to the actual labels:

model.score(x_train, y_train): Accuracy on the training data.

model.score(x_test, y_test): Accuracy on the test data.

These metrics help evaluate how well the model generalizes.

6.21. Summary:

This code builds and trains a Random Forest Classifier on training data **(x_train, y_train).**

Predicts labels for test data **(x_test).**

Computes accuracy on both training and test datasets to assess performance.

```
In [51]: # Printing the Confusion Matrix
         plt.subplots(figsize=(15,8))
         from sklearn.metrics import confusion_matrix

         # Creating a Confusion Matrix
         cm = confusion_matrix(y_test, y_pred)

         # Printing the Confusion Matrix
         plt.rcParams['figure.figsize'] = [5, 5]
         sns.heatmap(cm, annot = True, cmap = "Purples")
```

Fig- 6.27:-The above code visualizes a confusion matrix using a Heatmap.

Here's a breakdown of its components:

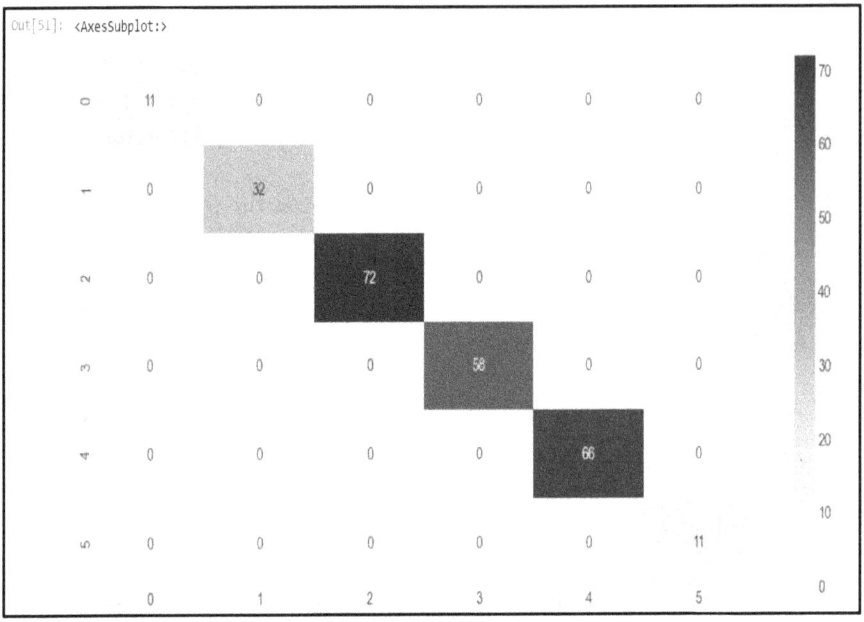

Fig: 6.28:-Creating Confusion Matrix using Heatmap for data visualisations

6.22 Creating Confusion Matrix using Heatmap for data visualisations

Code Explanation:

Code explanation

plt.subplots(figsize=(15,8))

This initializes a figure with a size of 15x8 inches for plotting. However, this line appears redundant because the size is later overridden with plt.rcParams.

from sklearn.metrics import confusion_matrix

Imports the confusion_matrix function from the sklearn library.

This function is used to compute the confusion matrix from actual and predicted values.

cm = confusion_matrix(y_test, y_pred)

Computes the confusion matrix using the actual values (y_test) and predicted values (y_pred).

plt.rcParams['figure.figsize'] = [5, 5]

Sets the figure size for the plot to 5x5 inches globally using Matplotlib runtime configuration settings.

sns.heatmap(cm, annot = True, cmap = "Purples")

Uses the seaborn library to create a Heatmap visualization of the confusion matrix:

cm: The confusion matrix to be visualized.

annot=True: Displays the values of the confusion matrix on the Heatmap.

cmap="Purples": Specifies the color palette to use (shades of purple in this case).

Purpose

The confusion matrix is a table used to evaluate the performance of a classification model.

Rows represent the actual class labels.

Columns represent the predicted class labels.

Each cell shows the number of occurrences of a particular combination of actual and predicted labels.

Key Points

Adjustments like plt.subplots are not necessary if the Heatmap size is controlled using plt.rcParams.

To avoid redundancy, remove or align the size configurations.

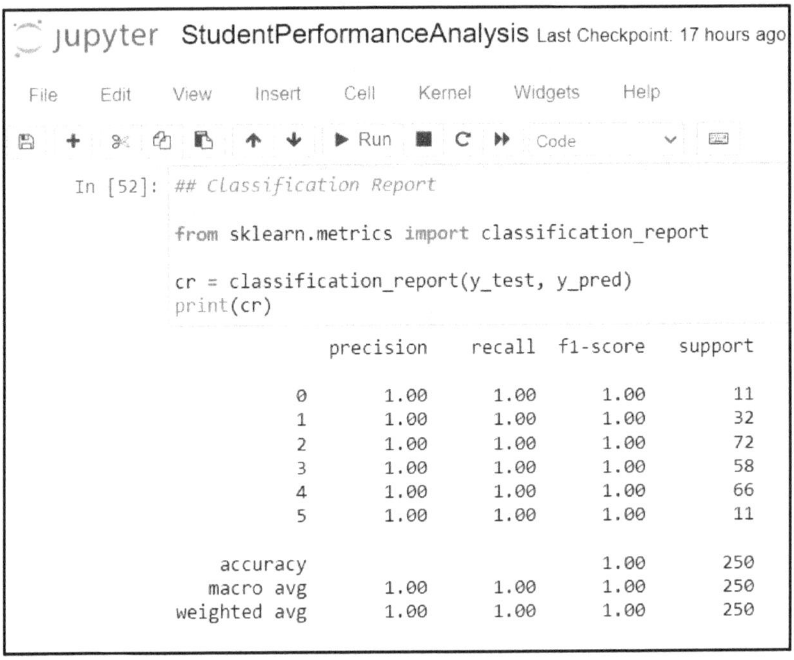

Fig: 6.29- Evaluating data using Classification Report

6.23 Creating Classification Report

Code Explanation:

The above code generates and prints a classification report, which provides a detailed evaluation of a classification model's performance. Here's a breakdown of the code:

from sklearn.metrics import classification_report

Imports the classification_report function from sklearn.metrics. This function computes a report summarizing the main performance metrics for classification tasks.

cr = classification_report(y_test, y_pred)

Creates a classification report by comparing the actual values (y_test) with the predicted values (y_pred).

The classification report function computes metrics for each class:

This helps to identify how well the model is performing for each class.

Classes (0 to 5): The report evaluates six classes.

6.23.1. Precision:

Precision is the proportion of correctly predicted positive observations to the total predicted positive observations.

The code measures how many of the predicted positives were correct.

Result - 1.00 for all classes.

6.23.2. Recall:

Recall (Sensitivity) is the proportion of correctly predicted positive observations to the actual positives.

The above code measures how many of the actual positives were correctly identified

Result - 1.00 for all classes.

6.23.3. F1-Score:

F1-Score is the harmonic mean of precision and recall, balancing the two metrics.

The code compute the harmonic mean of precision and recall

Result - 1.00 for all classes.

6.23.4. Support: The number of actual occurrences of each class in the dataset.

Overall Metrics:

Accuracy:

Accuracy: The overall proportion of correct predictions.

Result - 1.00 (perfect accuracy).

6.23.5. Macro Average:

Macro Avg: Average of the metrics across all classes (unweighted).

Averages precision, recall, and F1-score across classes, treating all classes equally

Result - 1.00.

6.23.6. Weighted Average:

Weighted Avg: Weighted average of the metrics, taking into account the number of instances (support) in each class.

Averages precision, recall, and F1-score across classes, weighted by the number of instances in each class.

Result - 1.00

This indicates a perfectly performing model for this classification task.

Chapter 7

Industrial Application

Industrial applications of work on student performance prediction analysis in examination

The student performance prediction analysis in examinations has significant industrial applications in various fields. By using machine learning and data analytics to predict student performance, institutions and organizations can optimize resources, personalize learning, and improve overall educational outcomes. This technology can be integrated with the existing educational system which will help the teachers and the educators to better analyse the student's performance and work in proper direction for the betterment in the child development.

Below are several industrial applications of such a project:

7.1. Education Technology (EdTech) Companies

Personalized Learning: EdTech companies can use performance prediction models to tailor educational content to individual students. Based on predictions, these companies can offer adaptive learning platforms that modify difficulty levels, suggest remedial materials, or challenge high-performing students.

Adaptive Learning Systems: Systems can dynamically adjust curricula based on predicted performance, ensuring that students stay engaged and are not overwhelmed or under-challenged [54].

Student Engagement Analytics: EdTech companies can use predictive models to monitor student engagement and provide targeted interventions, such as reminders or motivational strategies, when a student's performance is likely to drop[55].

7.2. Educational Institutions (Schools, Colleges, Universities)

Curriculum Development: Institutions can use performance prediction data to identify patterns of student success or failure in particular subjects or courses. This data can help improve curriculum design by focusing on areas that need more attention or introducing additional support in certain subjects.

Resource Allocation: Schools and universities can use predictions to allocate resources more effectively. For example, if predictions indicate that a large number of students are likely to struggle with a particular subject, additional tutoring resources or specialized instructors can be assigned [56].

Early Intervention Programs: Schools can identify at-risk students early by analysing patterns in their past performance and other factors (e.g., attendance, socio economic status). This allows institutions to intervene with tailored support programs, counselling, or mentorship before students fall too far behind.

7.3. Government and Educational Policy Makers

Strategic Planning for Education Reform: Policymakers can analyse large-scale student performance prediction data to identify systemic issues and plan reforms. For instance, if certain groups of students are consistently underperforming across multiple regions or institutions, this can trigger discussions on funding allocation, curriculum changes, or teacher training.

Resource Distribution: Governments can use predictive models to forecast student needs across districts and allocate educational resources, such as funding, to areas most in need. This can help improve educational equity and efficiency.

Longitudinal Tracking of Educational Outcomes: Performance prediction can help in tracking the effectiveness of educational policies over time, offering insight into whether certain programs are achieving their intended outcomes [57].

7.4. Corporate Training and Development

Employee Upskilling and Reskilling: Companies offering employee training programs can use student performance prediction models to identify which employees are likely to succeed in certain types of training, allowing them to tailor courses and provide additional support where necessary.

Talent Management: By predicting the performance of trainees or new hires in skill assessments or exams, companies can identify talent gaps and plan for targeted professional development programs, helping retain top performers and boost productivity.

Corporate Learning Platforms: Companies can implement predictive models to guide learners through their internal training systems, offering personalized paths based on past performance, skills, and future potential.

7.5. Data Analytics and AI Consulting Firms

AI-Driven Education Solutions: Consulting firms can provide AI-driven educational tools that analyse student data for predictive analytics. These services can be sold to educational institutions, EdTech companies, or even governments looking to improve educational systems.

Developing Custom Models: Consultants can develop customized student performance prediction models based on specific needs of clients (e.g., tailored for specific institutions or countries), optimizing the model's use in real-world scenarios.

7.6. Private Tutoring Services

Targeted Tutoring Programs: Based on predictive performance analysis, tutoring companies can offer personalized tutoring programs, adjusting the learning material to address specific weaknesses identified in students' predictions. This could improve the efficiency and effectiveness of tutoring.

Student Retention: By predicting which students are likely to benefit most from additional tutoring, companies can target their services more effectively, increasing the likelihood of student retention and success.

7.7. Online Education Platforms (MOOCs)

Predictive Analytics for Course Design: Platforms like Coursera, edX, or Udacity can use prediction models to determine which students are more likely to succeed or drop out of online courses. This can help in refining course structures, providing additional resources, or offering peer support to keep students engaged.

Automated Feedback Systems: Prediction models can be integrated into online courses to automatically provide feedback to students, informing them of their progress and suggesting ways to improve based on their predicted performance.

7.8. Learning Management Systems (LMS)

Improved Performance Monitoring: LMS platforms can integrate predictive models to monitor student performance in real-time and provide instructors with alerts when students are predicted to fail or struggle. This allows instructors to intervene proactively.

Data-Driven Insights for Teachers: LMS platforms can provide detailed insights and analytics about student performance trends, enabling teachers to adjust their teaching methods or focus on specific areas where students are underperforming.

7.9. Healthcare and Special Education

Predicting Needs for Special Education: Using student performance data, educational models can help predict students' future needs for special education resources, supporting early intervention programs that address learning disabilities.

Tracking Student Well-being: Predictive analysis of performance can also help in identifying students who may need psychological or counselling services due to performance-related stress or other issues affecting their education.

7.10. Learning Analytics Software Development

Development of Predictive Analytics Tools: Software developers can create specialized predictive analytics tools for schools and universities that offer a deeper understanding of how various factors (such as teaching methods, study habits, and attendance) impact student performance. These tools can be licensed to educational institutions as software-as-a-service (SaaS) products.

In conclusion the industrial applications of a project on student performance prediction are wide-ranging, impacting not only the education sector but also EdTech, government policy-making, corporate training, and AI consulting. The ability to predict student outcomes accurately can lead to more personalized education, optimized resource allocation, and overall improvements in learning experiences and achievement.